SAY IT.
TELL IT.
LIVE IT.

AN INSPIRING *and* UPLIFTING
52 WEEK DEVOTIONAL

J. DREW SHEARD, B.S., M. ED

U🦅P
Uriel Press

Uriel Press books may be ordered through booksellers or by contacting:

Uriel Press
1663 Liberty Drive
Bloomington, IN 47403
www.urielpress.com
844-752-3114

ISBN: 979-8-8861-2018-9 (sc)
ISBN: 979-8-8861-2019-6 (hc)
ISBN: 979-8-8861-2020-2 (e)

Library of Congress Control Number: 2023917748

Print information available on the last page.

Urial Press rev. date: 9/29/2023

Bishop J. Drew Sheard stands in front of the Kathryn Kuhlman pulpit at the historical Bonnie Brae House, where the catalytic fire of the Azusa Street Revival was first ignited (Los Angeles, CA). (Cover Photo Credit: Nathan Brown)

DEDICATION

I am grateful and most appreciative to my Lord and Savior, Jesus Christ, for all of His benefits toward me.

To my loving family, my beautiful and multi-talented wife, I am what I am because of your loving support. To my awesome children, Kierra (Jordan) and J. Drew. Your phenomenal support is absolutely incredible! I thank God for trusting me with you both! My wonderful grandchildren. Jacob and Kali. To my brother, Ethan (Gwenda), thank you for everything. Your profound strength and support will never go unnoticed. To my incredible sisters: Dorinda (Greg) and Cindy. To my cousins, Bernita and Karen, for having my back.

To the absolute greatest church family in the world: GEI, I love all of you!

Thank you, Sis. Vickie, for your incredible assistance!

This book is dedicated to my parents.

Bishop John H. and Mother Willie Mae Sheard They are forever in my heart!

CONTENTS

FOREWORD

Dr. W. Franklyn Richardson, Chairman,
The Conference of National Black Churches

A voice of fresh insight for these troubled times.

I am humbled by the opportunity to recommend this Epistle of Good News to the global Christian family and to those who are carrying an uncultivated seed of salvation in their hearts. The following pages collectively form an earnest, passionate, and profound missive to all people, born in the heart of a prayerful and faithful servant.

As Chief Prelate of the Church Of God In Christ (COGIC), the Most Reverend J. Drew Sheard is one of our most spiritually empowered, socially relevant, and biblically informed religious leaders. On the pages that follow, he has provided a road map for developing and practicing mature and relevant faith, especially during these uncertain and turbulent times.

Bishop Sheard provides fresh manna from on high for a maturing spirituality and a pathway for spiritual development. His gifts of sacred and pastoral insights are on full display in these devotionals. The richness of his exegetical skills provides a relevant application of his extensive biblical understanding. He takes the ancient texts and gives them practical relevance for every man, woman, boy, and girl.

In this collection of devotions, we can feel Bishop Sheard's passion for people and his love of "God in Christ." As you read this sequence of messages, you will experience the delicate weaving of a warm security blanket of hope as you confront the daily issues of these times. Be prepared to be inspired and spiritually impacted as you encounter these gems of inspiration.

The framework of this presentation provides a disciplined opportunity for the reader to incorporate basic biblical insights in a sequential weekly format, ultimately developing or renewing his or her Christian faith. It provides a supplement to weekly Bible study and Sunday worship. Here we have an inter-testament excursion into biblical truth intended to enrich our faith in Christ. Bishop Sheard uses the scriptures as a vehicle to communicate the whole truth of the human predicament, which he makes clear is salvageable by the grace of God. Both pastor and parishioner will discover illumination and inspiration encountering the engaging terrain of this insightful presentation. All who are blessed to engage in this profound work will find a companion to expanding knowledge of the Word of God. This book is a must-read for all people of faith. I hope you find it as nurturing as l have. There is a blessing waiting here for you!

INTRODUCTION

A process, in its most basic definition, is a sequence of stages or actions carried out to accomplish a specific goal. We start aiming for perfection as soon as we accept that Jesus is the Son of God, that He suffered death on the Cross, and that He rose from the dead after three days. I've said it before, and I'll say it again: sanctification is a process. Every believer has a responsibility to get closer to God, and it is the role of every pastor, along with apostles, prophets, evangelists, and teachers, to aid in that process.

Although there are many different ways that the process of sanctification takes place, comprehending God's Word for appropriate life application is the most crucial part of the process. Pastors speak to congregations about texts on different days of the week with the hopes that the ideas will be understood, remembered, and recited when necessary for success in life.

The weekly devotionals presented here are intended to serve as both a reminder of what God has said and as a tool for resolving life's challenges in a way that pleases God. As you read these pages, I hope they remind you that you can accomplish anything through Christ who strengthens you, that this is a journey, that we improve each day, and that we must be doers of the Word rather than merely hearers. Keep in mind that through the way we live, we show everyone around us who God is.

Along your life's journey you must Say It. Tell It. Live It.

May you be abundantly blessed!

J. Drew Sheard

A GOOD NAME

A good name is rather to be chosen than great
riches, and loving favour than silver and gold.

—Proverbs 22:1 (KJV)

*Reflection: There are many names by which
God's chosen are recognized.*

IN MODERN TIMES, A FAMILY NAME MEANS LITTLE MORE THAN THE NAME that designates someone as an individual who lives at a certain place at a certain time. Such has not always been the case. In biblical days, great stress was placed upon the names of individuals and places. The name of a person provided insight into his or her character and life. Perhaps both our secular lives and our spiritual lives would be greatly enriched if a greater emphasis were placed on the value and the significance of a good name. A person's name really stands for his or her character, reputation, and integrity.

Throughout scripture, we are warned against using the name of God carelessly. To use his name is to involve Him in both our conversation and activity. God does not want to be misrepresented by the careless use of His name. Likewise, a family should be vitally concerned about its good name. Rich indeed are the children who receive good names from their parents. Ecclesiastes 7:1 says, "A good name is better than precious ointment, and the day of death than the day of one's birth." The value of one's name should be maintained at all times.

It would be helpful to recognize and respond properly to the names that have been bestowed on us as the children of God and as the servants of the Lord Jesus. We are called beloved of God in Romans 1:7. Recognize that you are precious and called to be a saint. As children of the promise (Romans 9:9), we are recipients and beneficiaries of God's declarations. To be called a servant of righteousness mandates freedom from the law and sin (Roman 6:18). In the New Testament, we find several names or titles that are applied to us, which we should bear with gratitude, dignity, and honor.

We are called believers because of our faith, and it is by faith that we respond to the love of God as revealed in the person of Jesus Christ. Because of our faith, God justifies us, declares us righteous and gives to us positions of acceptance in His presence. We do not find acceptance in the presence of God on the basis of keeping the law or on the basis of our moral perfection. It is by faith that we please God, and it is by faith that we achieve significant goals in our Christian lives.

This Week's Objective:
Maintain your reputation (good name) by
daily rehearsing obedience to God.

A TORN ROBE AND A SHAVEN HEAD

At this Job got up and tore his robe and shaved his head. Then he fell to the ground in worship and said: "Naked I came from my mother's womb, and naked I will depart. The Lord gave and the Lord has taken away; may the name of the Lord be praised."

—Job 1:20–21

> **Reflection:** Trouble and suffering are facts of life and not always the result of sin.

MY DEAR FRIENDS, SOMETIMES WHEN TROUBLE OVERWHELMS, YOU JUST feel like losing it. Is there any good news for those who suffer? In times when trouble strikes, we need to take an inventory to see if there is any good news that can cheer our hearts and help us bear the burden of pain. Job serves as an example of someone who has gone through the most drastic turnaround in life, and yet the Bible says that he "retained his integrity." How should a Saint cope with suffering and trouble? Those who really have a relationship with God pray and trust Him.

Job is a dramatic illustration of someone who experienced great suffering and catastrophe, which was both undeserved and unexplained. Job was a blameless man in the eyes of God, in the eyes of others, and in his own eyes. Before this experience, Job and his friends believed suffering was the result of sin, and people who suffered must have sinned. Job never considered God sometimes puts us in situations to help us grow.

How will you handle trouble? Will it bring you closer to Christ? Will it turn you away from and against Christ? When suffering comes to us, we must hold on to the conviction that God is love, and that God is good. We must believe God always acts in conformity with his good character.

Several suggestions may be helpful to us as we consider the possibility of suffering in the future. First, let's get acquainted with Christ as Savior, Teacher, Friend, and Helper. Let's also study the example of Jesus Christ as He dealt with the pain and suffering of others.

Before suffering comes, we need to develop resources to assist us. Develop the daily habit of a quiet time, when we let God speak to us from His Word. Let prayer be a conversation with God in which we not only speak to him, but let him speak to us. Regularly participate in public worship, and allow God to use this time to draw us closer to him. Develop genuine Christian friendships with other members of the family of God so they can be the mediums of God's ministry to us when trouble comes. Expect the angels of God to come in our time of need. In the meantime, we must not be anxious about trouble, which may come in the future.

This Week's Objective:
Live under the leadership of the risen Christ
and in the power of the Holy Spirit.

AGAINST THE ODDS

For when we were yet without strength, in due time Christ died for the ungodly. For scarcely for a righteous man will one die: yet peradventure for a good man some would even dare to die. But God commendeth his love toward us in that, while we were yet sinners, Christ died for us.

—Romans 5:6-8

Reflection: Only God has the power to restore humankind.

IN THIS MATERIALISTIC AND MUNDANE SOCIETY IN WHICH WE LIVE, much value is placed on strength, riches, and intelligence. Charles Darwin, a noted anthropologist and the father of the theory of evolution, purported that survival rests in the hands of those who are most capable of surviving. The biblical record announces with poignant clarity who will reach the mark and gain the prize. When we were weak, without strength, and in a state of passive helplessness to deliver ourselves from sin, Christ died. God rises up and fights on the side of the weak, the disadvantaged, the oppressed, and the poor. God gives no preferential attention to the high and mighty, but He has earnest compassion for the meek and lowly and gives them victory.

We are all unfit in many ways. The apostle Paul says in Romans 3:23, "For all have sinned and come short of the glory of God." Romans 3:10 says, "for there is none righteous, no, not one." God removes through tests and trials of life the mental and spiritual inadequacies of the unfit. He enables all to follow closely the guidelines of divine discipline in order to be best qualified for both temporal and eternal survival. Therefore, the unfit ought to be more zealous knowing that for survival, endurance is necessary.

Jesus did not die so we might remain the low people on the totem poles. He died so we might have a chance, gain strength, achieve, so we might be called the sons and the daughters of God. It is true that John the revelator saw two crowds entering into the kingdom of God. The first crowd was the chosen nation, the expected ones. But they were not all who would inherit eternal life. John also saw a nameless host of underprivileged people who came up out of great tribulation. These are they who have washed their robes in the blood of the Precious Lamb. These may not be the strongest, smartest, or richest, but against all odds they made it.

This Week's Objective:
Recognize God has given you victory regardless of perceived shortcomings.

DROP IT AND RUN

Wherefore seeing we also are compassed about with so great a cloud of witnesses, let us run with patience the race that is set before us.

—Hebrews 12:1–2

Reflection: God has enabled us, therefore we are winners.

As Christians, we often become easily discouraged and are tempted to slow down or to give up. Many hindrances thwart Christian progress: fleshly indulgence, faithlessness, lack of dedication, inordinate pride, and laziness. Drop those things and run. Jesus is the one who prepares the way for a person to be right with God. He is a constant companion to help us on our journeys.

The author of the book of Hebrews encourages believers to work on their stamina, saying, "Let us run with patience the race that is set before us." The encouragement to run with patience is interesting. Patience to many people means a calm resignation. This is not the meaning in the New Testament. There, the word translated means the determination to master something. Each of us must "press toward the mark for the prize of the high calling of God in Christ Jesus" (Philippians 3:14).

One of the real battles of running is a psychological struggle. In the mind of every runner, the temptation to quit is always present. However, "You were taught, with regard to your former way of life, to put off your old self, which is being corrupted by its deceitful desires; to be made new in the attitude of your minds; and to put on the new self, created to be like

God in true righteousness and holiness" (Ephesians 4:22–24). The runner must fight feelings of fatigue, the possibility of failure, and thoughts about the success of the competition. Nothing should stop the runner from completing the course.

The words, "Wherefore seeing we also are compassed about with so great a cloud of witnesses" reminds us that there is a legacy of those who have already run the Christian race. These people gave testimony to the worthiness of their faith in the Lord. They finished the race with their faith intact. Why is this so important? Runners are inspired by other runners. Witnesses inspire Christians to be faithful. Witnesses testify to the power of faith.

The Christian life is a foot race. To run effectively in a foot race, impediments must be removed, the course needs to be mastered, the crowd needs to inspire, and endurance needs to exist. Staying with the Christian life has many benefits. First, we have the joy of running the race. Second, we can see the accomplishment. Third, the Christian receives the crown. How well are you running today?

This Week's Objective:
Strive in faith to be victorious.

I AM IN NOW

But now in Christ Jesus you who once were far off
have been brought near in the blood of Christ.

—Ephesians 2:13 (KJV)

Reflection: All of humanity has been gifted access to God.

IN THIS SCRIPTURE, PAUL GRAPHICALLY PORTRAYED THE REALITY OF
alienation. Those who choose not to live life with God suffer from a life
apart from God. This choice makes them strangers to the Lord. Being a
stranger does not mean that God arbitrarily cuts certain individuals off
from Himself. Being a stranger simply means that simple human rebellion
has separated a person from God in this life and in the life to come.

When the news about the Gentiles accepting Jesus began to spread,
it was a great disturbance to the Jews, who felt the Gentiles were inferior
to the Jews in religious privileges. Paul reminded the Gentiles that they
once sought admission into the kingdom of heaven in vain. He states in
Ephesians 2:12, "You [Gentiles] were at that time separated from Christ,
alienated from the commonwealth of Israel, and strangers to the covenants
of promise, having no hope and without God in the world." But Christ
made the difference. The sole reason for the Gentiles' admission was the
character and work of Jesus.

Christ did a marvelous work of reconciliation, which brings access.
Ephesians 2:18 says, "For through him we both have access in one Spirit to
the Father." The new relation is pictured as an access or right of approach.
Christians have the privilege of access to God as children do to a loving

father. Gentiles may have been left out before, but they are now a part because Jesus made a way.

Receivers of Christ's reconciliation become insiders. Metaphorically speaking, strangers become citizens of God's country, children in God's family, and integral parts of a structure. Jesus gave the Gentiles a sense of belonging. Ephesians 2:19–20 tells us, "So then you are no longer strangers and sojourners, but you are fellow citizens with the saints and members of the household of God, built upon the foundation of the apostles and prophets, Christ Jesus being the cornerstone." Together with Jewish believers, Gentiles form the true Israel of God.

Jesus Christ is the focal point for both Jewish believers and Gentile believers; Christ Jesus is the cornerstone. Do you want to be in the kingdom of God? If the answer is yes, you must come through Jesus Christ, because apart from Him we are outsiders. Jesus makes the difference.

This Week's Objective:
Open your heart to Jesus Christ and become an insider.

MOMENTS OF WEAKNESS

Esau said to Jacob, "Feed me, I pray thee, with that
some red pottage; for I am faint:" therefore was his
name called Edom. And Jacob said, "Sell me this day thy
birthright." And Esau said, "Behold, I am at the point to
die: and what profit shall this birthright do to me?"

—Genesis 25:30–32 (KJV)

Reflection: Weak moments are inevitable.

T HE WEAKNESSES OF PEOPLE HAVE CAUSED MANY TO GO TO THEIR
graves with untapped or unused resources. Men and women who have
the potential to leave great marks in history are brought to nothing more
than another person because of weakness. Each of us experience weak
moments during which we should never make decisions.

Esau allowed physical impulses to dictate his actions, and he lived to
regret his carelessness. Esau was hungry and tired, and his brother Jacob
was cooking his favorite dish: red stew. Under one condition could Esau
have the stew: he would have to sell his birthright. When we allow our
physical appetites to reign, we always make matters seem worse than they
really are. These are the times when our resources are depleted. Our focuses
shift to the temporal, and we zero in on satisfying the particular appetites
that are nagging us, giving little heed to the consequences. It is not worth
it to solve short-term dilemmas at the cost of long-term possessions.

Esau had a marvelous privilege that he never could have attained
through human achievement. Unfortunately, he disdained his gift during

a moment of weakness. Feeling the pains of hunger caused him to treat his privilege carelessly. Gifts are not to be taken lightly. God endows all believers with one or more gifts, and He greatly desires that we acknowledge and use those gifts.

Perhaps the greatest lesson Esau learned is the crucial importance of moments of decision. We should be ever conscious of God's leadership during our moments of strength and during our moments of weakness. If we look to Him for guidance, He will never lead us to regret a decision.

Many Christian brothers and sisters are on the verge of becoming extraordinarily used by God, but they can't control their desires. Don't give up your future for a moment of pleasure. All of us have those times of weakness and we need help from someone greater than ourselves. That someone is Jesus.

This Week's Objective:
Don't be caught up in a single fleeting moment;
there is something better up the road.

PROCLAIM THE GOSPEL

The word that came to Jeremiah from the Lord, saying,
Stand in the gate of the Lord's house, and proclaim there
this word, and say, Hear the word of the Lord, all ye of
Judah, that enter in at these gates to worship the Lord.

—Jeremiah 7:1–2 (KJV)

"The Spirit of the Lord is upon me, because he hath
anointed me to preach the gospel to the poor; he
hath sent me to heal the brokenhearted, to preach
deliverance to the captives; and recovering of sight to
the blind, to set at liberty them that are bruised."

—Luke 4:18 (KJV)

Reflection: Every Christian has a responsibility
to share the Good News of Jesus.

WHEN CONTEMPLATING SOCIETAL ISSUES, THERE IS USUALLY A gathering of secular minds and ideologies, but lives cannot be changed by simple words or a strong thought. We must resort to that which has been proven when we speak of life-changing solutions and preparing the souls of men and women for the life hereafter. Let us observe that the proclamation of the Gospel is one of certainty, is unwavering in its authority, and has been proven to work.

The early Christians went everywhere proclaiming the gospel of Jesus Christ. What imparted such authority to their message in the face of all sorts of adversities and refutations? Upon what foundations do we find a sure footing as we proclaim the gospel to a world flooded with lost souls? It is the foundation of great and abiding theological truths that time and eternity shall never change. We can be sure that what the real Church has proclaimed thus far is an unchanging gospel based on a theological foundation that no person can lay but the man Christ Jesus.

God's condemnation of sin and unrighteousness still stands firm today. It is up to us, the Church, to proclaim the righteousness of God. Hebrews 9:27 says that it is appointed unto people once to die, but after this is the judgment. Death is only a doorway to the unavoidable life beyond. We have a responsibility to tell the world that death is not the end. The Bible says inextricably that the wages of sin is death, but the gift of God is eternal life.

The command to spread the Gospel is very clear and the unchanging authority of God's word assures the proclaimer of success. The Bible says to all of us, "Go ye into all the world and preach the gospel to every creature." There is work to be done and we must realize that there is a pressure of duty laid upon us and we cannot stop working. Somebody needs to know that Jesus is the light of the world, that the Lord will forgive them of their sins, and that they can make it.

This Week's Objective:
Tell someone about Jesus today.

RISKY BUSINESS

Therefore said he unto them, The harvest truly is great, but the laborers are few: pray ye therefore the Lord of the harvest, that he would send forth laborers into his harvest. Go your ways: behold, I send you forth as lambs among wolves.

—Luke 10:2–3 (KJV)

Reflection: Opposition is innately a part of working in the Kingdom of God.

OST OF US DO NOT LIKE TO TAKE RISKS IN LIFE; WE WOULD MUCH rather deal with safe issues. However, life is a great risk, and so likewise proclaimers of the gospel are risk takers. We must set out with an expectation of trouble and persecution, for Jesus said, "Behold, I send you forth as lambs among wolves; but go your ways, and resolve to make the best of it." Our enemies will be as wolves, but we must be as lambs, peaceable and patient. Even though we are made easy prey, be wise, because he or she who wins souls must be wise. Soul-winning and church work is risky business, but taking a risk for God will pay off.

In Luke we find, seventy disciples being sent two by two into difficult and challenging situations. Their mission was to be witnesses of Jesus and to work miracles in the places He instructed them to visit. You and I have likewise been given assignments by the One who controls the world, and as many soldiers as possible are needed to combat the hands of the enemy.

Being called to do the work of the Lord is not necessarily as glorious as some make it appear. We are challenged on a regular basis. Sometimes, it looks like the devil is winning, but God would not send us out to lose.

Be encouraged and know that Jesus labor was not in vain. Although He met with opposition, He was still effectuating change.

There are many reasons why people do not come to the point of believing Jesus is Lord and joining the Church. Could one reason be that we have not accepted the empowerment given by God to go out into the world and reach the lost? If so, take the risk and act upon the mandate given by Jesus to "Go out and seek." Recognize and understand that there is a risk attached to the business of saving souls, but there are also blessings from God for those who will take the risk and compel men and women to be saved.

This Week's Objective:
Tell those you come in contact with about Jesus.

THE BUSH IS YET BURNING

And the angel of the Lord appeared unto him in a flame of
fire out of the midst of a bush: and he looked, and behold,
the bush burned with fire, and the bush was not consumed.

—Exodus 3:2 (KJV)

> **Reflection:** *God will work through those
> with willing and obedient hearts.*

WHEN ISRAEL'S DELIVERANCE OUT OF EGYPT WAS PROMISED TO Abraham, he saw a burning lamp, which signified the light of joy that deliverance would cause. Then there appeared an angel of the Lord to Moses, an extraordinary manifestation of the divine presence and glory of a Holy God. Now the light of joy shines brighter, as a flame of fire. Moses heard God speaking and calling him to a higher job. God in deliverance brought terror and destruction to His enemies, gave light and heat to His people, and displayed His glory before all.

Whenever the Lord calls us to do a job, we must not consider our own personal affinities or natural attributes. We must be sure we have willing and ready hearts. Moses began to think about his insufficiencies for the task. He began to feel and think of himself as unworthy of the honor. When a person looks at his or her abilities and measures them by the yardstick of human capabilities, that person will always find excuses. God uses His own standard of measurements, which always makes up for the shortages in our lives and makes us adequate for whatever the tasks might be.

If we will be the instruments through which God will speak, we must pull off the things of this world. When we have messages from the Lord, it is imperative that we walk worthily and adhere to his admonitory counsel. Moses left the business he was attending to and took special note of the burning bush. God took note of Moses' inquisitiveness and spoke from the bush. Moses returned an answer of obedience: "Here am I, what saith my Lord unto his servant." Moses expressed his reverence and his readiness to obey. God told him to "put off thy shoes from thy feet for this is holy ground."

There is still a voice speaking from the burning bush today. The Church has been commissioned. God is calling us to rescue a dying world. Our assignment is more important than being President of the United States, and greater than being a dictator to the world, because it involves setting the captive free. Satan's slaves are floating on the escapades of worldly preferment. The Lord is saying to the Church, "Throw out the lifeline because someone is drifting away." The commission we have received tells us to demand freedom from the oppressor. For this cause, we must work and never allow the bush to go out. Thank God there is no end to this bush, no end to His voice, and no end to our God.

This Week's Objective:
Answer the call of God; you have work to do.

THE DAY THAT THE LORD HAS MADE IS A DAY TO REJOICE

This is the day the LORD hath made; we
will rejoice and be glad in it.

—Psalms 118:24 (KJV)

*Reflection: The works of God provide
many reasons to give praise.*

THERE ARE SEVERAL SPECIAL DAYS WE LOOK FORWARD TO DURING THE year by the Church. We remember God's works and wonders of old, while at the same time acknowledge the value of the present and the promise of the future. Let us look at things that can help us to rejoice on a daily basis.

Remember the Lord's mercies and be thankful, praising God in the darkness and the storm, as well as in the light and the calm. Lamentations 3:22–23 says, "The steadfast love of the Lord never ceases, his mercies never come to an end, they are new every morning, great is your faithfulness." It has been said, "We forget the mercies as soon as they are past, because we only enjoyed the sweetness of them while they were in our mouth." To rejoice and be glad, we must recognize not only what the Lord has done, but also what He is doing.

Remember the prayers God has answered. In the latter part of Psalm 118:5, the writer states, "The Lord answered me, and set me in a large place." In fact, in Isaiah 65:24, the Lord said to Isaiah, "Before they call,

I will answer; and while they are yet speaking, I will hear." It is good to know that God is yet listening to us and answers our prayers.

Remember to learn from your past. Know your limitations, identify your weaknesses, accept the counsels of prudence from your failures, and control your ambitions by remembering it is the Lord's purpose that prevails. As we read in Romans 15:4, "For whatever was written in earlier times was written for our instruction, so that through perseverance and the encouragement of the Scriptures we might have hope." For your soul's sake, get the poisons of the past out of your system and rejoice.

Remember to recognize opportunities. The wise person makes the most and the best he or she can of that which is within reach and that which is before his or her face. Our prayer should be: Lord, may I never surrender to one of life's locked doors. Instead, may I use the keys on the key ring of prayer until I find the right key and the door is opened.

Every day, we can rejoice when we remember God's works, His mercies, that He answers prayers, and that we have grace to learn from our pasts and to recognize opportunities. One day at a time, let us declare what the psalmist said centuries ago: "This is the day which the Lord hath made; we will rejoice and be glad in it."

This Week's Objective:
Make it a daily habit to remember God's benefits and rejoice.

THE HOUSE THAT WORSHIP BUILT
(WRITTEN BY KAREN CLARK SHEARD)

"After this I will return, and will build again
the tabernacle of David, which is fallen down; and
I will build again the ruins thereof, and I will set
it up: That the residue of men might seek after the
Lord, and all the Gentiles, upon whom my name is
called," saith the Lord, who doeth all these things.

—Act 15:16–17 (KJV)

"But the hour cometh, and now is, when the true
worshippers shall worship the Father in spirit and in
truth: for the Father seeketh such to worship him."

—John 4:23 (KJV)

*Reflection: A house of true worship is always
ready for the presence of God.*

THERE ARE MANY HOMES THAT CLAIM TO BE SPIRITUALLY BUILT BUT worship is a missing component. Worship stabilizes, purifies, and sets the foundation of a house, bringing the building process to completion. Our scripture in Acts describes the need for restoration of the place where God resides and where His name can be called upon. In this passage, God once again volunteers to assist David in restoring to people passion and desire for Him. When we allow our houses to be built by worship, we have the assurance of God's presence.

David pursued the presence of God. He was a God-chaser and a man after God's own heart. The reason some of us cannot get to the next dimension in God is our pursuit of material things. The Bible says, "Seek ye first the kingdom of God and His righteousness and all these things shall be added unto thee." If we seek God concerning His house, He will bless us with the things we need in our houses.

The Holy Spirit does not dwell in an unclean temple. Let us remove the dust of self-righteousness from the mantles of our hearts and disinfect areas in our lives that hold us back from worship. Straighten the wrinkled drapes in our minds so that we are prepared for action, keeping a clear head and setting our hopes on the grace to be brought to us at the revelation of Christ.

A house built by worship gives a sense of security. We know we can resist what the enemy sends our way. We become caught up in God's presence and He gives us the power to endure and to command the devil to take his hands off our lives. We learn to use trouble to fuel our worship. God becomes bigger than our problems and He makes our enemy to be at peace and bless us.

This lesson is not about a mechanical reproduction of David's tabernacle; this is about a rebirth of passion and dedication of our life to God. We are building places not for God's benefit but for the benefit of the one who builds the house according to God's habitation and expectation. God will not prove Himself to be Jehovah-Jireh-God our provider, Jehovah-Rapha-God our healer, and El Shaddai-God almighty.

This Week's Objective:
Purpose to live in a house built by worship so that you may know God.

THE JOURNEY OF LOVE

And Rizpah the daughter of Aiah took sackcloth, and
spread it for her upon the rock, from the beginning of
harvest until water dropped upon them out of heaven,
and suffered neither the birds of the air to rest on
them by day, nor the beasts of the field by night.

—2 Samuel 21:10 (KJV)

Reflection: Love never fails.

LOVE IS THE MOTIVATIONAL FORCE BEHIND THE FULFILLMENT IN LIVING. As the redeemed of the Lord, we know that our redemption was provided through love. John 3:16 says, "For God so loved the world that he gave his only begotten Son, that whosoever believes in him should not perish but have everlasting life." Love is God's nature implanted in us. Love shines the brightest, love endures the longest, love carries the most hope, and finally, love remains forever.

Rizpah had been the concubine of King Saul. Two of the men who were hanged in Gibeah were her sons. Her heart was shattered as the horses leapt forward and the ropes gripped tightly around the necks of her sons. What Rizpah does, however, defies belief. The bodies are cut down and left to decompose; they are denied a decent burial in order to set an example. For 150 days, Rizpah guards the remains of the seven sons of Saul. Her ears listen every night for the footsteps of the jackal or some other scavenger. Her sunburned face scans the heavens so she can scare away the vultures. The bones of the seven were bleached white in the sun, yet she stood guard as her gift of love. Only love could provide this kind of motivation, only love could force this kind of determination, only love could furnish this kind of resolution, and only love could go this far.

I want to remind you of love's longest journey. Love had never taken a trip like the one it took when the eternal Son of God, who was butchered and bleeding, ascended the hill of the skull. There He was poured out like water for a dying, sin-sickened humanity. Every drop of blood and every bead of sweat showed His unfathomable love.

Love will find a way, for it goes farther, reaches higher, delves lower, and sings sweeter than anything else. Tongues will one day cease and knowledge will vanish as the morning fog, but love never fails and love will forever remain. Love brought us out, love dusted us off, love picked us up, and love turned us around. That's the true journey of love.

This Week's Objective:
Live your life loving unselfishly.

THE PRACTICE OF GIVING

Therefore, as ye abound in every [thing, in] faith, and
utterance, and knowledge, and [in] all diligence, and [in]
your love to us, [see] that ye abound in this grace also.

—2 Corinthians 8:7 (KJV)

Reflection: *Received blessings are to be shared.*

G IVING SHOULD NOT BE SEEN AS A BURDEN OR BECOME A SUBSTITUTE
for other kinds of Christian service. It is the responsibility of every
Christian to participate in the grace of liberality. Throughout biblical
history, from the tithing system of the Old Testament to the communal
giving in the early church, there was a requirement that people give back to
God a portion of their money. The Church must encourage people to work
hard, manage wisely, and keep all financial gains available to God's touch.

The willingness of believers to give generously to God is linked to
one's own prosperity. Proverbs 3:9-10 says, "Honour the Lord with thy
substance, and with the firstfruits of all thine increase: So shall thy barns
be filled with plenty, and thy presses shall burst out with new wine." In
studying the history of the Jewish people, their prosperity could always be
measured by their offerings to the work of the Lord. In other words, their
finances measured their religion. If the children of Israel were so willing
and generous in their giving under the first covenant in Exodus 36:5–6,
what should the Christian do under a better covenant? When God's people
appreciate the grace revealed in Christ and become partakers of His divine
nature, they possess a spirit of unselfishness and liberality. Let us observe

Acts 2:45 and 4:34–35. God is the greatest of givers. Those who have been born of Him take on the characteristics of their heavenly Father. Their time, wealth, abilities, and influence are willingly and cheerfully given back to Him who first gave to them.

Jesus used language that left no doubt as to what should be done with the blessings of life, whatever they may be: spiritual, physical, or material. He taught that as the blessings of life are received, they are to be shared so that others may become recipients of better and more meaningful things. In so doing, we give meaning, direction, dignity, and value to life. This is stewardship at its best.

The real purpose of stewardship is not to raise money but to develop strong Christian character. Christian stewardship is the acknowledgment of possessions and the administration of the same according to the will of God. We must continue to teach God's financial plan and the duty of each individual to practice that plan.

This Week's Objective:
Manage the finances entrusted to you by God
according to His giving principles.

THE THREE DIMENSIONS OF LIFE

And the city lieth foursquare, and the length is as large as the breadth; and he measured the city with the reed, twelve thousand furlongs. The length and the breadth and the height of it are equal.

—Revelation 21:16 (KJV)

Reflection: *Life at its best is complete on all sides.*

JOHN THE REVELATOR, IMPRISONED ON A LONELY, OBSCURE ISLAND called Patmos, was deprived of every convenience imaginable except he was able to use the freedom to think. He thought about the old Jerusalem and its superficial piety and its perfunctory ritualism. John also had a glorious vision of something new and great. He saw a new and holy Jerusalem descending out of heaven from God.

The most notable thing about this new heavenly city was its completeness, radiant as daybreak ending the long night of stagnating incompleteness. It would not be partial or one-sided, but complete in all three of its dimensions. In describing the city, John says, "The length and the breadth and the height of it are equal." The new city of God would not be an unbalanced entity; it would be complete on all sides.

In our individual and collective lives are a disturbing incompleteness and an agonizing partialness. Almost every affirmation of greatness is followed, not by a period symbolizing completeness, but by a comma punctuating its nagging partialness. Many of our greatest civilizations are great only in certain aspects. Many of our greatest people are great only in certain ways and are low and degrading in other regards. Yet life should be strong and complete on every side.

Any complete life has the three dimensions suggested in our text: length, breadth, and height. The length of life is the inward drive to achieve one's personal ends and ambitions, and inward concern for one's own welfare and achievements. The breadth of life is the outward concern for the welfare of others. The height of life is the upward reach for God. Life at its best is a coherent triangle. At one angle is the individual person. At the other angle are other persons. At the tiptop is the Infinite Person, God. Without the due development of each part of the triangle, no life can be complete.

Every person must have a concern for self and feel a responsibility to discover his or her mission in life. God has given each normal person a capacity to achieve completeness. Some are endowed with more talent than others, but God has left none of us talentless. Potential powers of creativity are within us, and we have the duty to work assiduously to discover these powers. After one has discovered what he or she is made for, he or she should do it as though God Almighty called him or her at this particular moment of history for this reason.

This Week's Objective:
Discover what you are made to do, and then give
yourself passionately to the doing of it.

THE WAIT IS OVER

In these lay a great multitude of impotent folk, of blind, halt,
withered, waiting for the moving of the water. For an angel
went down at a certain season into the pool, and troubled the
water: whosoever then first after the troubling of the water
stepped in was made whole of whatsoever disease he had.

—John 5:3–4 (KJV)

Reflection: *God is the giver of new and marvelous things.*

W E NOTE THAT GOD HAS BROUGHT ABOUT CLOSURES IN THIS YEAR
and we are expecting the completion of more things and the
beginning of better things. We do not always understand what God is
doing in our lives, however in His infinite wisdom, He views our total
picture. We can only reflect on the past, live out the present, and anticipate
the future, but God can see the past, the present and the future all at the
same time. Therefore, it behooves each of us to adhere to His words and
trust our journey to His perfect will.

The Feast of Pentecost signified the completion of seven complete
weeks and one day after the Passover. Bethesda was a spring-filled pool
located on the northeast side of the city by the sheep gate. Bethesda literally
means "House of Mercy," but there was absolutely nothing merciful-
looking about that place. Bethesda was actually a sad sight because we can
see a multiplicity of misery and heartache. Crammed around this pool were
impotent, blind, halt, and withered people in need of a miracle. They sat

there, lay there, or were propped up at the pool looking for the angel to come and stir the water so they might jump in.

The people at Bethesda had been waiting for days, months, even years, and in their stories, we see described for us a perfect picture of today's world. All we have to do is look around in our communities and we will find people who are dissatisfied with their conditions and are anxiously waiting for situations to change. This world is filled with people who are afflicted but cannot save themselves. They see others receiving miracles and it seems like they will never come close to receiving their breaks. But the wait is over. Get ready—your help is on the way. Jesus issues the same challenge that he did to the man by the pool of Bethesda to us today: "Wilt thou be made whole?" Do you want to be complete? Do you want to do better? Do you want to be helped?

This encouragement is for those who are ready for a new beginning. You are saying, "Enough is enough" and are willing to allow God to bring closure to your old way of life and pursue newness. Get up and start walking in destiny. Move from lethargy into a season of productivity and step out of spiritual dullness into a fresh anointing and a rich relationship with God. Isaiah 42:9 says, "Behold, the former things are come to pass, and new things do I declare." God is up to something great. It's time for revelation and manifestation.

This Week's Objective:
Start rejoicing over new victories.

THE URGENCY OF REPENTANCE

Seek ye the Lord while he may be found, call ye upon him while he
is near: Let the wicked forsake his way, and the unrighteous man
his thoughts: and let him return unto the Lord, and he will have
mercy upon him; and to our God, for he will abundantly pardon.

—Isaiah 55:6-7 (KJV)

Reflection: *Christ will judge us on the basis of our decision.*

G OD IS AVAILABLE TO THOSE WHO CALL ON HIM AND ARE CONCERNED
enough to turn to him. "The Lord is nigh unto all them that call
upon him" (Psalms 145:18). We must be earnest if Christ is to be found
as our Savior. "Ye shall seek me, and find me, when ye shall search for me
with all your heart" (Jeremiah. 29:13). A person does not reluctantly or
inadvertently become a Christian. God is available right now to all who
are sincere about coming to Him.

Unfortunately, vast numbers of men and women have an attitude of
lethargy toward their spiritual condition. God does not promise to be
available tomorrow. Having itching ears we have been lulled to sleep by
false teachers. We are drugged with moral laxity, spiritual indifference, and
blind obsession for the approval of people. We are in a spiritual stupor and
have lost all sense of the urgency of repentance.

The Bible classifies us as "wicked" and "unrighteous" and clarifies the
penalty of sin in Romans 6:23, "The wages of sin is death". Is there a way
out, is there a solution? The answer is yes—repentance. Isaiah 44:7 defines
repentance beautifully. In repentance, a person turns from (forsakes) sin,

turns to God (returns unto the Lord) and receives forgiveness (He will abundantly pardon).

The urgency of repentance arises from the imminency of Christ's return which forever seals our decision. "But of that day and hour knoweth no man, no, not the angels of heaven, but my Father only" (Matthew 24:36). Christ came the first time as Savior, but when He comes again it will be as Judge.

This brief life is infinitesimal compared with eternity and we are afforded sufficient opportunities to repent while we live on earth. After a person dies, judgement comes and all will live in eternity. The question is not whether one lives after death but rather, where one lives after death.

This Week's Objective:
Ask for forgiveness swiftly.

THIS THING IS SERIOUS!

Then I said, I will not make mention of him, nor speak any more in his name. But his word was in mine heart as a burning fire shut up in my bones, and I was weary with forbearing, and I could not stay.
—Jeremiah 20:9 (KJV)

Reflection: What is God's call for your life?

BECAUSE OF THE ANOINTING THAT IS UPON OUR LIVES, THERE ARE going to be times when we will experience unnecessary criticism, be misunderstood, and be mistreated. The call of God is not to be taken lightly and there are tough times ahead. We must remember that even though difficulties come our way, and we feel like throwing in the towel, we cannot quit.

Jeremiah was a threat to the authority of Pashhur, especially since this priest thought so much of himself that he added prophecy to his duties. Pashhur was angered beyond control at Jeremiah, and hit him with his open hand. Jeremiah was not only restrained and tortured but he was put in the stocks at the upper Benjamin Gate, which was one of the city's most conspicuous places. In other words, Jeremiah was made an open spectacle so that the public would discredit his ministry. Pashhur released Jeremiah, thinking that he had taught him a lesson, only to find out that Jeremiah had not changed his message.

Nowhere else in scripture is a prophet's sense of divine compulsion to his mission so clearly expressed. Jeremiah never doubted the reality of his call and never lost his identity under God, but yet he became discouraged.

He never questioned the authenticity of the call that was upon his life, but yet he became discouraged. Jeremiah claimed that the Lord overpersuaded him to be a prophet. He pleaded that, though the Lord overcame his resistance to his call, and he believed the Lord's promises, he had now been abandoned to shame. However, the Lord had clearly informed Jeremiah of the difficulties he would face. It is, however, understandable, that he would not have conceived the magnitude and viciousness of the opposition.

Jeremiah learned the calling that was on his life was irreversible and that God's word was irrepressible. Likewise, the call of God that is upon your life can only be effectuated through acceptance and obedience. Once you make the decision to yield to God's plan, your name may be plastered on the billboard of scandal. Traps may be set for you, but stand firm. Always remember Luke 9:62: "But Jesus said to them, No one after putting his hand to the plow and looking back, is fit for the kingdom of God." This thing is too serious to just walk away.

This Week's Objective:
Live as an ambassador for God in whatever situation the Lord assigns to you.

WHAT SHOULD I DO NOW?

And he said, While the child was yet alive, I fasted and wept: for I said, Who can tell whether God will be gracious to me, that the child may live? But now he is dead, wherefore should I fast? Can I bring him back again? I shall go to him, but he shall not return to me.

—2 Samuel 12:22–23 (KJV)

Reflection: We are a part of a culture that fails in how we handle death.

ERSPECTIVE IS EVERYTHING, ESPECIALLY IF YOU PLAN TO LIVE LIFE TO its fullest. Our viewpoints become warped when death makes a sudden, unanticipated, or anticipated for that matter, visit to our families. We either over spiritualize death or become extremely cavalier. At death, some people canonize (declare to be a Saint) their worst family members because they refuse to admit the possibility of their eternal loss, or they become angry at God for taking their loved one away. Others sit around to see what they can get as a result of a death. If we allow ourselves to fall apart over any crisis, we risk losing the benefits of experience afforded us by each circumstance.

While King David attended to his child who was sick for a long time, he prayed for healing, failed to eat, lamented, and did not perfect his own body. But the day came when the child died. The strangest thing happened when servants admitted to David that the child was no longer alive. He got himself up from the floor, stopped crying, and took a bath. David put on cologne, got dressed up, and went to church to worship.

When church ended, David replenished his strength with wholesome nourishment because he needed to get on with the business of living.

What we do when things fall apart is stay at home where all of our fears, pain, and hurts develop and mature. King David knew to conquer these feelings, he needed to change scenery and get a new perspective. I know this doesn't sound good or make sense in times of death, but God is in control and God never makes a mistake.

I wish that our culture could redefine the way we prepare for the burial of loved ones. David's staff saw how he acted, called the king aside, and asked him about this unusual behavior. He gave them a most classic answer for how we should handle death: "But now he is dead, why should I fast? Can I bring him back again? I shall go to him, but he shall not return to me."

What should I do now? The obvious answer is to know Jesus Christ in the pardon of your sin and be filled with His Spirit. It is the only way that you can be assured of having peace in the life hereafter. How you go is most important.

This Week's Objective:
I admonish those of us who are left behind to seek God.

WHEN GOD SAYS IT, AGAIN

God spake unto Moses, and said unto him, I am the Lord.

—Exodus 6:2 (KJV)

Reflection: *God will do exactly what He promises.*

YOU NEED TO HEAR FROM GOD WHEN THE ENEMY COMES AGAINST YOU. Even though you have God's assurance of help, sometimes you need reassurance of what God has said to you. Moses was greatly discouraged over the opposition of Pharaoh, but God came to bring him a great reassurance. He promised that Moses would see God at work against Pharaoh. Fighting the enemy and standing for God often causes weariness. The disciple Paul said in Galatians 6:9 that it is possible to be "weary in well doing." When we become weary, we have a tendency to doubt, so we need God's reassurance.

Remember who God is and remember His majesty. God's name discloses His character and brings reassurance. Exodus 6:3 says, "I appeared unto Abraham, unto Isaac, and unto Jacob, by the name of God Almighty, but by my name Jehovah was I not known to them." God Almighty, in Hebrew *El Shaddai,* means mountain God. In this name, there is the feeling of fear and trembling in the face of God's overwhelming majesty. Nothing brings greater assurance than a new sense of awe about God's greatness and insight into the majesty of God.

God reassures us by His covenant and faithfulness in the past. He has never renounced one of His promises. When God makes a covenant, He will be faithful. Much of the Christian's assurance is from the promises of God. Let us trust the covenant that God has made with us. He will do exactly what He said.

God's reassurance does not come with a promise of an easy road. He forecasts obstacles and hindrances, but He gives a challenge to obey Him, regardless of anything. One of the ways to combat opposition is to proclaim faithfully the Lord's will.

Are you discouraged in your work for God? Has persistence in doing good made you tired? Has the lack of response caused you distress? If so, start anticipating what God will do. God promised to redeem you, bring you out, rid you of your enemies, and be your God.

God's people have a great future. God has made bountiful assurances of what is ahead for the Christian. He has made great promises about life on earth and even greater promises about life after death.

This Week's Objective:
God can encourage you and bring great comfort.
Listen to him say, "I am the Lord."

WHEN IT'S TOO LATE, IT'S JUST TOO LATE

They went into the ark with Noah, two and two of all
flesh in which there was the breath of life. And they that
entered, male and female of all flesh, went in as God
had commanded him; and the Lord shut him in.

—Genesis 7:15–16 (KJV)

Reflection: God always provides a way of escape.

THE ONE WHO MADE THE WORLD WILL NEVER TURN IT OVER COMPLETELY to the forces of evil. He didn't do it in Noah's day, and He is not going to do it in our generation. Those who believe in God and commit themselves to His requirements will find security when the Day of Judgment arrives.

God is patient, for He wishes no one to perish, but He also comes to the point when He can't wait any longer for people to repent. The Day of Judgment always arrives. Beyond a doubt, Noah will remain forever one of the greatest preachers who has ever lived. He saw the course that events were taking and, perceiving the inevitable consequences if those things continued, could not keep silent. With his heart overflowing, he became a preacher of righteousness.

Even though God's judgement is inevitable, He provides a way for humankind to receive undeserved blessings. As John 3:16 states, "For God so loved the world, that he gave his only begotten Son, that whosoever believeth in him should not perish, but have everlasting life."

Consider Noah's children; were they genuine converts? There are different thoughts that exist with reference to their spiritual conditions. Perhaps they simply believed their father and lived according to his prophetic counsel and God, through His mercy, spared them. Whatever view we take, one thing stands out succinctly: We often receive a blessing from being in the right place at the right time. Shem, Ham, and Japheth were in the household of Noah. Either directly or indirectly, deserved or undeserved, this allowed them to participate in the blessing of being delivered when the great Day of Judgment came to the earth.

Genesis 7:16 is one of the most significant verses in the entire flood story. It says, "And they that went in, went in male and female of all flesh, as God had commanded him: and the Lord shut him in." Of course, God protected Noah, but the verse contains a warning to every unrepentant sinner who is in the process of turning down the call of God. The shut door excluded those who refused Noah's message and consigned them to a watery grave. There was no further opportunity. The door of mercy had remained open for one hundred and twenty years. Then it was closed.

This Week's Objective:
Get into the ark of safety; the next judgement is coming by fire.

A BAD DECISION COSTS A PROMISING FUTURE

But he went in, and stood before his master. And Elisha said unto him, Whence comest thou, Gehazi? And he said, Thy servant went no whither...And he went out from his presence a leper as white as snow.

—2 Kings 5:25–27 (KJV)

Reflection: An eternal perspective yields good life choices.

L IFE CONSTANTLY REQUIRES DECISIONS RELATING TO OUR HUMAN needs, and the pressures can be relentless. In spite of this fact, our spiritual sensitivity must remain keen so that our vision is sharp when making choices and giving service to God. The wrong perspective can lead to failure in fulfilling your God-ordained destiny.

Gehazi was the obvious choice to fulfill God's plan for succession in replacing an aging Elisha. He was experienced and more qualified for the office of prophet than Elisha had been when he served as the apprentice to Elijah. So what went wrong? Gehazi performed good deeds, yet this did not save him in his hour of temptation. Gehazi made a bad, destiny-altering decision in securing a temporal reward over eternal recompense.

The doctrines of God's word are the anchor of our faith. This means it is impossible to formulate spiritual and honorable decisions without knowing, believing, and applying God's perspective. Ensure that you know what God thinks by reading your Bible regularly.

Gehazi had knowledge of Elisha's position on accepting gifts from Naaman, the captain from Syria's army, but knowledge was not enough. Even when it is known what God says about something, in order to avoid making a bad decision, wisdom must be exercised. Wisdom is acquired by "hearing counsel (listen), and receiving instruction (accept discipline)" (Proverbs 19:20). Are you listening to God and doing what He says?

In John 15:5, Jesus teaches that abiding with Him is critical to decision-making processes that lead to successful outcomes: "He that abideth in me, and I in him, the same bringeth forth much fruit." God is always with you, but make sure you are maintaining a set time to come into His presence.

Gehazi's unfulfilled promise was avoidable, and it is important that we learn from his disastrous error. An eternal perspective can be maintained if we abide with God through faith, spend time in His presence, and be intentional in our actions to please Him.

This Week's Objective:
Treasure above all else your destiny in the Kingdom of God.

A BETTER PLACE

These all died in faith, not having received the promises, but having seen them afar off, and were persuaded of them, and embraced them, and confessed that they were strangers and pilgrims on the earth…But now they desire a better country, that is, an heavenly: wherefore God is not ashamed to be called their God: for he hath prepared for them a city.

—Hebrews 11:13–16 (KJV)

> **Reflection:** The promise of heaven gives us the strength to keep going.

THE BIBLICAL SCRIPTURES REVEAL OUR HOME AS A HEAVENLY PLACE. It is called by a variety of names or significant appellations: the Habitation of God, Glory, My Father's House, New Jerusalem, the City of God, and Paradise. However you may refer to that heavenly place, it is a better place than this present world. Close your eyes and imagine a place that has no sin within all of its borders. The streams of water are all pure, the sky is cloudless and radiant, and the air is unimpregnated with pollution. God is everywhere and the refulgent rays of the divine holiness spread through all the extent of that heavenly place. The atmosphere is untainted by human offences. There is not a disease incidental to that much better place. The air is salubrious, the enjoyments without peril, and the food incorruptible; therefore, sickness is unknown. Can you see it? By faith, believe and be strengthened as you live out your life in this present world.

The weight of just living is not always easy to bear, and neither should we expect it to be. We are often distressed through our own infirmities as well as those of others. Some people are possessed with uninformed understanding, some have unsound judgment or stubborn dispositions, and still others have wayward or hasty tempers. In this present world, we must righteously deal with it all as we pursue happiness and purpose.

Do not allow people to make you believe that everything you need is in this life. This world is full of God's goodness, but the richer blessings are in that better heavenly place. Believe, keep the faith, and know that Jesus has made preparations for all who would do His will in our measured duration of time in this present world. Our obedience automatically prepares us for a better heavenly place.

This Week's Objective:
Keep heaven in your view.
Make up your mind to go all the way to the end with God.

A MISSION MADE POSSIBLE

Not by might, nor by power, but by my Spirit, saith
the Lord of hosts. Who art thou, O great mountain?
Before Zerubbabel thou shalt become a plain.

—Zechariah 4:6–7 (KJV)

Reflection: *Spreading the good news of Jesus is the responsibility of every Christian, but God does the real work.*

T HE CONVERSION OF SOULS TO GOD IS AN OBJECTIVE SO MOMENTOUS that, under any circumstances, it is worthy of every effort to render it attainable. However, it is vain to attempt to accomplish this task by human power and might. Regardless of the skill and energy of man these things can never bring about a great moral renovation in the world. Let it then be observed that human power, in and of itself, is quite insufficient to effect conversion of the soul to God. Yet, in establishing God's spiritual kingdom among mankind, you and I have been given the command to go into all the world and preach the gospel to every creature.

The great work of converting and purifying souls belongs exclusively to God and to Him is ascribed the first awakening of the soul. Therefore, the instrument employed for converting this heathen world is peculiarly God's own. It is the Word of God only which works effectually in the soul.

Carnal reasoning suggests there is no necessity to attest to the lifechanging power of God, but each of us must silence every objection to this idea. Let us excite ourselves to fresh, unwearied ardor by continually looking up to God for strength as we witness. Second Corinthians 3:5–6 says, "Not that we are sufficient of ourselves to think anything as of ourselves; but our sufficiency is of God; who also hath made us able ministers of the new testament; not of the letter, but of the spirit: for the letter killeth, but the spirit giveth life."

This writing is calculated to elevate our hopes of success as we press forward daily in compelling people to accept Jesus as their Savior. Every child of God must promote the interests of saving souls, never forgetting that it is not by might, nor by power, but by the Spirit of the Lord that humankind is converted. It's the anointing that sets us free.

We are endeavoring to spread the gospel and build up the church of Christ. Our cause is a great cause, but our challenges are many. Let us always keep in mind that God is an all-sufficient God and heaven rejoices with the conversion of one single soul.

This Week's Objective:
Be ready to give an answer to every person who asks why you have hope.

WHATEVER!

The words of the Preacher, the son of David, king
of Jerusalem. Vanity of vanities, saith the Preacher,
vanity of vanities; all is vanity. What profit hath a man
of all his labour, which he taketh under the sun?

—Ecclesiastes 1:1-3 (KJV)

Reflection: *A sincere heart devoted to God is priceless.*

SOLOMON ASCENDED TO THE POSITION OF KING AS THE SON OF KING David, but because of his sin, Solomon broke peace with God and lost the peace of his conscience. Solomon eventually took an inventory of himself and realized his conduct was dishonorable to God. He also became desirous of redirecting back to God those whom he may have led astray. God has regard for true repentance, and because Solomon acted accordingly, he became the preaching soul, expressing the sentiment recorded in our reference scripture. Every individual needs to take an inventory, ascertain how often they have done things to dishonor God, and do whatever is necessary to be in right standing with the heavenly Father.

What is it that Solomon has to say through the writing of the book of Ecclesiastes? He aims at making us truly religious and taking away our esteem and expectations from the things of this world. The things that we seek after are impertinent to the soul and add nothing to mankind's proposed ultimate destiny of heaven. All is vanity. Solomon speaks to us as one having experience and authority, not only as that of a king but also as that of a prophet and a preacher. Solomon was divinely inspired by God.

Solomon teaches that the things of this world are insufficient to make us happy. He comes to this conclusion through our subject, or, in modern terminology, whatever! We have come to use the word "whatever" to imply that something is not of substance or that we really don't care about the outcome of the situation to which we connect the word. If we talk about money, power, or influence, it does not phase the rich King Solomon, whatever! Or if we talk about women, it does not phase King Solomon with all of his wives and concubines; whatever! Solomon seeks to appeal to mankind's conscience. He understands the constant fatigue associated with worldly business and how it wearies us.

Luke 12:15 says, A man's life consisteth not in an abundance of the things which he possesseth." All he or she gets will not supply the wants of the soul nor satisfy its desires without God. Things will not atone for the sin of the soul or cure its diseases. What profit will these things be to the soul in death, in judgment, or in that everlasting state? The fruit of our labor in the world is only meat that perishes, but the fruit of our labor in heavenly things is meat that endures to eternal life.

This Week's Objective:
Respond to things that pull you away from God with — Whatever!

AGGRAVATED IN CHURCH

And her adversary also provoked her sore, for to make her fret, because the LORD had shut up her womb. And she was in bitterness of soul, and prayed unto the LORD, and wept sore.

—1 Samuel 1:6, 10 (KJV)

> **Reflection:** *God is the answer even when we are faced with exacerbating circumstances.*

THOSE WHO ATTEND CHURCH NEVER ANTICIPATE BEING AGGRAVATED by fellow churchgoers. We expect church to be a place where the wounded, sad, or depressed come and not only receive comfort from the Lord but encouragement from fellow attendees. Because there has been general decay and neglect of true religion, the reasons people attend church are varied and may not be reflective of a sincere desire to worship God. Regardless of this reality, we must remember God is available to those who seek Him.

Elkanah was a man in the Bible who had two wives. One wife, Hannah, was barren and criticized by the other wife Penninah, who envied the interest Elkanah had in Hannah. It was very unkind of Penninah to annoy Hannah when it was God's time to be worshipped. Hannah grew melancholy and discontented, Penninah grew haughty and insolent, and Elkanah was stuck in the middle of it all. Additionally, Elkanah had to deal with unscrupulous individuals who claimed to be in ministry but conducted themselves in a very nonreligious way. These issues did not stop Elkanah from attending church. Whatever others did, he resolved that he and his house should serve the Lord. He went up out of his city yearly to worship and to sacrifice unto the Lord of hosts in Shiloh.

You may be in a place of depression, be troubled, and be tormented by fellow churchgoers, but your agenda is to meet God in His house. Hannah could not take the vexing of her righteous soul during worship by Penninah. Even though Hannah was resentful, she prayed to the Lord while she cried. The resolution of Elkanah and the response of Hannah to irritation in church are examples we can all follow when being aggravated by others at the time of worship. Keep seeking God; He is the one who can change our circumstances.

Eventually, Eli the priest recognized Hannah's dilemma and pronounced, "Go in peace and may the God of Israel grant your request." God answered Hannah's prayer in spite of Penninah's behavior, and He will respond to each of us as we cry out to Him and worship. God sees everything and He has not forgotten you. Continue to pursue God no matter what, and the time of blessing will come.

This Week's Objective:
Determine in your heart that you will let nothing
separate you from the love of God.

AN INVITATION TO DESTINY

And the same day, when the even was come, he saith
unto them, Let us pass over unto the other side.

—Mark 4:35 (KJV)

Reflection: Obtaining destiny often involves
transitioning through stormy weather.

IN PURSUIT OF OUR DESTINIES, WE ARE GOING TO BE HIT BY STORMY weather, but we should remember Jesus is on board. When the disciples' and Jesus got into a boat, a violent windstorm came. The waves were breaking into the boat so that it quickly filled up with water. It is said that this tempest arose not by chance or by the power of Satan but by divine providence for the trial of the faith of Christ's disciples. First Peter 1:6–7 says, "Wherein ye greatly rejoice, though now for a season, if need be, ye are in heaviness through manifold temptations: That the trial of your faith, being much more precious than of gold that perisheth, though it be tried with fire, might be found unto praise and honor and glory at the appearing of Jesus Christ."

There will be times in our walks with Christ when we should be able to pass elementary lessons and graduate to higher levels. In preparation for the next move, God is taking time to straighten us out on issues in which we have been negligent. The new level may not be easy to obtain and the journey could get rough. However, I encourage you to accept the invitation to pass over to the other side and transition to the next dimension.

The devil planted in the disciples' spirits that he was going to kill them and they said, "Master, carest thou not that we perish?" Jesus got up, rebuked the wind and said to the sea, "Peace, be still." The wind ceased and there was a great calm. Recognize your storm has been divinely sent, in the same manner that it was for the disciples. Know that the devil will be on hand to attempt to destroy you, but God will be in the midst of the storm and show His supremacy.

Go through your stormy journey with the knowledge that destiny is on the other side. Never relinquish the truth that there is nothing God cannot do. Peter said, "Beloved think it not strange concerning the fiery trial as though some strange thing has happened unto you, but rejoice and be glad." Are you ready for this? If so, accept God's invitation to destiny.

This Week's Objective:
Hear the Lord saying that this storm is going to make you better.

ENEMIES OF THE FAMILY

Be very careful, then, how you live—not as unwise but as wise, making the most of every opportunity, because the days are evil.

—Ephesians 5:15–16 (KJV)

Reflection: Obedience to God's word protects the family.

WE SHOULD BE AWARE OF THE ENEMIES OF THE FAMILY THAT CAUSE the bond of trust to become frayed and broken. While it is true that the influence of non-Christian minds can be detrimental to the health of the family, this is not our primary enemy. The real enemy of the family arises out of disobedience to the Word of God. The family is lost when no one sets standards for Christian attitudes toward life. Beware of the enemies that seek to destroy your family. Ask God to help you defend against permissiveness, drunkenness, selfishness, carelessness, and ignorance.

A permissive attitude is popularly expressed through sexual immorality and perversity. Christians walk in love, as taught by Christ. Parents can demonstrate a consistent Christian lifestyle along with administering fair and loving discipline to help protect their family from this enemy.

A family is severely frustrated when one of its members becomes enslaved to drunkenness. Address alcohol and drug problems aggressively and immediately using both spiritual and natural resources. Warnings against drunkenness include not only the indulgence in wine, but all liquors and drugs that alter the mental and emotional state and make us vulnerable to temptation and evil.

Marriage is a blending of lives and both husbands and wives are to be respected and loved. Submit to one another out of reverence for Christ and be concerned about each other's welfare, self-esteem, and future. Selfishness is the enemy. Thinking of one another and doing loving things for one another are ways to overcome this enemy.

Likewise, parents are advised not to provoke their children to anger. This means, obviously, that discipline must be fair and just. It also means that parents must not be careless of their children. When parents don't listen, set boundaries, show interest, or expect excellence, children experience deep anger. Be available to offer support to your children at the times in their lives when it can bring joy and growth.

Finally, the greatest strength in any home is the knowledge of the Lord. If you must, confess that you are ignorant of God's ways and do not know the Lord well enough. God invites you to start to walk with Him in faith that you may indeed be wise and successful in making the most of the time you have with your family.

This Week's Objective:
God wants us to continually grow in the fullness of life in Jesus Christ.

FROM VICTIM TO VICTOR

And he saith unto them, "Be not affrighted: Ye seek
Jesus of Nazareth, which was crucified: he is risen; he
is not here: behold the place where they laid him."

—Mark 16:6 (KJV)

Reflection: Overcoming sin and death
is God's promise to the believer.

O NE THING WE MUST LEARN ABOUT LIFE IS THAT INTERRUPTIONS AND
interferences can alter our plans. However, never forget that by the
resurrection of Jesus Christ, defeat is turned into victory. The message
went out that Jesus was dead, and the Jewish authorities believed Jesus
would still be lying in the tomb when they returned from observance of the
Sabbath. However, their expectation was not realized. The Son outshined
the sun. Jesus got up with unmistakable power in His hand. The apparent
defeat of the cross at the resurrection became an open door to life.

Recognize that you are not a victim. As stated in Deuteronomy 20:4,
"For the Lord our God is the one who goes with you to fight for you
against your enemies to give you victory." When defeat is turned into
victory, we have an affirmation of life, which is the continuing presence of
Christ. How do we know that Christ is alive? We have the evidence, and
furthermore we can feel Him all over and around us.

It looked like defeat was certain for Jesus when they crucified Him,
but three days later, the victim became the victor. Jesus Christ is the
only founder of a world religion who died and rose from the grave. The
resurrected Christ gives victory in the midst of struggle, hope in a world

of darkness, and meaning to life. The resurrected Christ takes the sting out of death and gives confidence in the face of death.

Because of the resurrection of the living Lord, you and I have life, and authorization to spread the word proclaiming the message of victory. Through the lives that we live, serving and trusting God, each born-again believer declares victory over sin and death. First John 5:4 reads, "For whatsoever is born of God overcometh the world: and this is the victory that overcometh the world, even our faith." God has authorized each one of us to speak life in authority and without fear, regardless of the circumstance. We have been authorized to proclaim that the Savior is risen and that we were once defeated but He gave us victory.

This Week's Objective:
There is new meaning to life, and our lives have
been turned around because we met Jesus.

GOD'S PROPERTY

But you are a chosen race, a royal priesthood, a holy nation, God's own people, that you may declare the wonderful deeds of him who called you out of darkness into his marvelous light.

—1 Peter 2:9 (KJV)

Reflection: We are God's peculiar people, His property, for His purpose.

To SAY WE ARE GOD'S PEOPLE IS TO REMIND OURSELVES THAT SOME DO not belong to Him. That does not mean they were not created by God or that He does not love them. It simply means that some are not willing to come to Him, surrender to His will, and accept His love. They may go to Hell, but they can never go unloved. We can all be God's people, but we must be willing to respond to His call.

God has chosen us that we may declare the strong, virtuous, and wonderful deeds of our Savior. He calls us to be His people that we may share aloud the glory of His deeds done on our behalf and the radiance of the light that has penetrated our darkness. When the power of those mighty deeds surge through our hearts, we are able to witness to a cynical world with lips and lives that are eager expressions of the joy and victory that have claimed us in Jesus Christ.

Because of His love for us, God did not send a substitute to do what He had to do Himself. It took a God who was both human and divine, who understood our struggles, and at the same time had a remedy for our survival. God held nothing back and has committed Himself wholly that we might be His people. The King James Bible translates the phrase "God's own people" into "a peculiar people." The old Latin word *peculium* referred to property. The proper translation is not that we are an odd people, but rather we are God's property.

Having met the requirements and becoming the perfect sacrifice, is it any wonder that when the God who gave Himself asks for our commitment, He asks not for substitutes but for our very selves? He now calls us to commit ourselves to declare His wonderful deeds and marvelous light to a world in darkness. The one question that remains is, will we permit God's commitment to shape the nature of our commitment?

We may experience many kinds of pain, tests, and trials in our Christian walks, but God is not willing that any should perish. To all who believe, He has given power to become the children of God. Always remember you belong to God.

This Week's Objective:
As God's property and remembering your commitment
to Him, declare His glorious deeds.

THE CUTTING EDGE

Be content, I pray thee, and go with thy servants. And he
answered, I will go. So he went with them. And when they
came to Jordan, they cut down wood. But as one was felling
a beam, the axe head fell into the water: and he cried, and
said, Alas, master! for it was borrowed. And the man of God
said, Where fell it? And he shewed him the place. And he cut
down a stick, and cast it in thither; and the iron did swim.

—2 Kings 6:5–6 (KJV)

*Reflection: God's anointing gives victory
and makes room for more.*

JESUS IS CALLING FOR US TO TEAR SATAN'S KINGDOM DOWN. WE NEED
soldiers who are armed and dangerous and ready to fulfill the assignment
of our Captain. As soldiers, we must be willing to face the enemy using the
specific piece of artillery needed to accomplish this feat: God's anointing.

The anointing places us in authoritative positions. As soldiers, we
recognize the fire of the Holy Ghost is required to burn up the bulrushes
of sin. Many people have access to the gospel but not everyone has the
anointing. We need that cutting edge to destroy yokes and cut down the
things that are not like Christ. Satan will not get out of the sinner's way
through philosophical teaching and analytical deductions. Urban projects
and governmental initiatives won't change the hearts of the wicked.
Transcendental meditation will not block demons from infiltrating minds.
However, the anointed gospel of Jesus Christ will, so we point a hopeless
world to a Savior filled with hope.

In the referenced Bible verses, students of Elisha the prophet were gleaning information to become better prophets. As the number of students increased, the learning space became too small. While working at chopping lumber down, one of the men lost his axe head. It was a disheartening thing for him because he knew he could not successfully do the work without his cutting edge. Those of us who work for the Lord should do it with fierceness. However, you and I ought to be concerned about trying to do the Lord's work without the anointing. Elisha cut off a piece of wood, threw it into the water and made the ax head float. God's grace can summon your lost anointing and cause your heart to settle its affections on things above.

Protect your edge and use what God has given you to put the devil in his place. Walk in your God-given authority and let Satan know that his time for reigning is up. The anointing gives an edge over all enemies and makes us bold soldiers.

This Week's Objective:
Continue to fight the good fight of faith.

I'VE GOT TO GET
BACK TO BETH-EL

Then God said to Jacob, "Arise, go up to Bethel and dwell there; and make an altar there to God, who appeared to you when you fled from the face of Esau your brother." And Jacob said to his household and to all who were with him, "Put away the foreign gods that are among you, purify yourselves, and change your garments. Then let us arise and go up to Bethel; and I will make an altar there to God, who answered me in the day of my distress and has been with me in the way which I have gone."

—Genesis 35:1–3 (KJV)

Reflection: *Only in God can we find peace and safety.*

IF WE ARE TRUTHFUL, ALL OF US MUST ADMIT THAT MANY DIFFERENT things have happened to us since our first experiences with God. Have you drifted from where you were when you first believed? Has the fervor of your salvation diminished? Has the god of mammon led you down the path of destruction, where materialism caused you to abandon your best benefactor? Would you rather take a chance on an attractive individual who makes you feel good as opposed to depending on the one who said, "I will never leave you nor forsake you"? Many people have allowed the vicissitudes of life to cause them to stray from serving God in the way they know they should. God stands with his arms stretched open wide, saying you can always come back home.

The life of Jacob was one long struggle. He was always in a position where he had to contend and scheme for what appeared to be success. It was at Bethel that Jacob had the assurance of God's protection and realized that the very thing he was worried about had already been worked out. The prophet Isaiah said, "Let the wicked forsake his way and the unrighteous man his thoughts: and let him return unto the Lord, and he will have mercy upon him; and to our God, for he will abundantly pardon."

We all must come to a point of return. We have listened to the prophecies go forth. We have been warned, caveated, and admonished. Let us take note of ourselves. We have taken the blessings of the Lord for granted. Also, we have drifted toward spiritual neglect, self-indulgence, and permissiveness. Additionally, we have aligned with a world that denounces the very foundation of decency and has become desensitized to the anointing of God. However, there remains a place where we can feel secure in an insecure society and sense the anointing of the Holy Ghost.

If we get back to Bethel, our fears can be calmed, our worries can be eradicated, and the strongholds of the enemy can be loosened. My prayer is; "Lord work on me, search me, fix me, cleanse me, sanctify me, baptize me, anoint, and revive me."

This Week's Objective:
Build God an altar.

LAUNCH OUT INTO THE DEEP

Now when he had left speaking, he said unto Simon, Launch out into the deep, and let down your nets for a draught.

—Luke 5:4 (KJV)

Reflection: *There is great benefit in responding to God's commands with faith.*

IT IS DIFFICULT TO EXPLAIN THIS MATTER OF FAITH, WHERE IT COMES from and how faith comes at a particular moment in time. The Apostle Paul understood that faith is a mysterious mixture of that which is both human and divine. He spoke of saving faith in Ephesians 2:8–10: "For by grace are ye saved through faith; and that not of yourselves: it is the gift of God: not of works, lest any man should boast." According to this passage we must conclude two things. First, God is the prime mover in this matter of faith. His grace is ever-present to help and to assist us. Second, faith is not without the human element and we must play our roles as well.

Jesus said to Simon, "Launch out into the deep, and let down your nets for a catch." Not only was Simon a fisherman, but we have every reason to believe he was a very skilled fisherman. Jesus of Nazareth was a carpenter. More pressing in the light of this interaction, Simon understood that there were times when fishermen did not catch fish. Therefore, the command may have seemed foolish to him. Simon made excuses by saying, "Master, we have toiled all the night, and have taken nothing." How easily we determine that God's commands or requests are irrational and without meaning. God never gives foolish commands.

We may not say so, but deep in our hearts we begin to doubt, concluding that the Father really does not understand our situations. Sometimes, we act as though God does not know what He knows and we presumptuously communicate the facts of a situation based on our humanistic perspectives. We give faithless answers, maintaining attitudes that fail to take into consideration that Jesus can do anything but fail. For you and me, faith remains a possibility. To forget this truth leads to despair. Hope may be dim and the possibilities may seem utterly beyond all expectations, but we must not give up. We must be able to see beyond our circumstances and ignore what the prognosticators say, always remembering we walk by faith and faith can bring the unexpected miracle.

I would like to suggest at least three ways each of us can launch out. Give ourselves to fervent prayer and do not stop praying. Too easily we forget the power of this mighty weapon. Next, willingly make ourselves and all our resources available for the Lord's service. Jesus still honors our acts of submission as acts of faith and uses them as bases for miracles. Finally, we must live out our faith. God wants and expects us to put faith into action.

This Week's Objective:
When God speaks, always respond with faith.

A PRAYER FOR THE KNOWLEDGE OF HIM

For this cause, I bow my knees unto the Father of our Lord Jesus Christ, of whom the whole family in heaven and earth is named, that he would grant you, according to the riches of his glory, to be strengthened with might by His Spirit in the inner man; that Christ may dwell in your hearts by faith; that ye, being rooted and grounded in love, may be able to comprehend with all saints what is the breadth, and length, and depth, and height. And to know the love of Christ, which passeth knowledge, that ye might be filled with all the fullness of God.

—Ephesians 3:14–19 (KJV)

> **Reflection:** God's work brings glory in the Church now and forever.

THE FIRST PRAYER IN OUR CITED SCRIPTURE IS FOR SPIRITUAL revelation, "That ye may know." Walk as far as you desire, and you will never walk beyond the boundaries of the depth, height, breadth, and length of the love of God. God's love is wider than any ocean, deeper than any sea. It was His love that captured us from a degraded world of sin.

The capacity of God's love is conveyed in the words "to know," which means to comprehend. As you grow not only in grace but also in the knowledge of the Lord, you have more capacity for His love. God will respond by pouring more love into your heart. Romans 5:5 says, "And the hope maketh not ashamed; because the love of God is shed abroad in our hearts by the Holy Ghost which is given unto us."

The second prayer in the referenced Scripture is for spiritual realization: "That ye may be." The Apostle Paul petitioned each believer to yield to the indwelling power of the Lord by His Spirit. Paul anxiously prayed that God's people understood God's work in their souls.

The consequence of realizing that Christ lives within us should be the manifested presence of Christ's love. Let us note the confirmation of that love. In Galatians 5:22, the Bible says, "The fruit of the Spirit is love." When saints know not only their commitment to the Lord but also the Lord's commitment to them, they willingly submit their lives to the Lord's love. When you really know that Christ loves you, then you lose your suspicions and are "rooted and grounded" in love, which means learning to trust and obey the Lord.

Think of the magnitude of the truth that the Lord Jesus lives in each believer's life. Having the knowledge of God's love is a great honor. Having that same love alive in us is a privilege with a price that cannot be measured. Jesus, the Son of God, lives in his people by the Holy Spirit. Colossians 1:27 states, "To whom God would make known what is the riches of the glory of this mystery among the Gentiles; which is Christ in you, the hope of glory."

This Week's Objective:
Endeavor to live your life in love, for God is love.

AFTER A MEETING WITH JESUS

What wilt thou have me to do?

—Acts 9:6 (KJV)

Reflection: *The conversion of sinners is always a marvel.*

THE PERSON WHOSE TRANSFORMATION EXPERIENCE IS PRESENTED IN Scripture was one of the most unlikely prospects for Christianity ever known to humankind. He had one of the most dynamic, far-reaching conversion experiences in the annals of history. His name was Saul. The Bible tells us that Saul did everything he could to persecute the saints. He was pushing in the wrong direction. Acts 9:1–2 says, "Then Saul, still breathing threats and murder against the disciples of the Lord, went to the high priest and asked letters from him to the synagogues of Damascus so that if he found any who were of the Way, whether men or women, he might bring them bound to Jerusalem." Saul doubted that Jesus was the Messiah, and his doubt drove him to attempt to eradicate the spread of the gospel.

The hand of God struck powerfully, facilitating a confrontation with the human heart of Saul. Suddenly, there was a light from heaven, Saul fell to the ground and heard a voice say, "Saul, Saul, why are you persecuting Me?" He said, "Who are You, Lord?" Then the Lord said, "I am Jesus whom you are persecuting." A change is seen in Saul. The Bible notes, "So he, trembling and astonished, said, 'Lord, what do You want me to do?'" Up until this submission, Saul had been doing what he liked, what he thought best, and what his will dictated. After the submission, he was told what to do. What a change in direction.

Examine the present human race and you will find twenty-first-century people are guilty of pushing in the wrong direction, as can be seen in their self-indulgence. This is especially manifested in the use of drugs and alcohol, in the practices of illicit sex, and in the increasing emphasis on materialism. Human beings of this era are going in the wrong direction as seen in confirmed unbelief and rejection of Christ. The state of indecision and procrastination on the part of many is pulling them in the wrong direction with fervor. I pray that people will lose the scales that are on their eyes, turn and be converted, and become witnesses that Christ is the Son of God.

Any of us who becomes a Christian must have a similar experience as Saul. Occasionally, someone will have a vision or some unusual or remarkable experience that will confront him or her. But more often, the words of a saintly witness given in either a personal way or in a public address are the means by which a person is saved. A true mark of a conversion experience is sharing the Good News with others. It is the duty and privilege of all believers to tell others about the saving power of the Lord Jesus.

This Week's Objective:
Prepare for a life of ministry and share the Good News of Jesus Christ.

GETTING GOOD OUT OF BAD

But I would ye should understand, brethren, that
the things which happened unto me have fallen out
rather unto the furtherance of the gospel.

—Philippians 1:12 (KJV)

Reflection: *There is great benefit and opportunity
in suffering for the cause of Christ.*

AILED PLANS, SICKNESS, SHATTERED DREAMS, THWARTED OPPORTUNI-
ties, death—all these can cause us grief, yet they may also lead to tremendous opportunities. Paul longed to go to Rome to preach the Gospel. He did go to Rome, but he was there as a prisoner. He made use of his time by writing letters to the churches. Paul's personal situation was bad because he was imprisoned. But his spiritual situation was good because he was preaching the Gospel in Rome. Paul's shining example serves as a source of inspiration for all saints.

While we suffer hardship, others can see the reality of God in our lives. A physician relayed to a group of friends how she had come to meet Jesus, whose power to save transformed her life. One of the steps that led her out of the atheism she once boasted was the manner in which a young Christian husband and his wife received a great disappointment. "It was a hard thing to tell them," she said. "I knew how they had longed for children to gladden their hearts and now their hopes were blasted. But it was the way they took it that impressed me. I know that God was real to them. I was haunted by the realization that they had something I did not possess—and I wanted it." God's power can make good come out of any situation, no matter how bad it may seem.

Let us pray for each other that we are able to see the hand of God in every situation. Paul was dependent on the prayer of fellow Christians. He was able to say, "For I know that this shall turn to my salvation through your prayer." Intercessory prayer is one of the great privileges of the Saints. We can pray for strength for one another, and we can pray that the bad circumstances in which other Christians find themselves can be used for good.

Those around you are viewing your suffering and deprivation as you share your source of strength in the person of Jesus Christ. Your display to others will witness to the character of a true Christian. Use every opportunity to be a witness for Christ as your personal Savior. Each time something happens that is unfavorable to you, give God glory through your testimony of knowing that no matter what, God is going to bring you out.

The motive for getting good out of bad is that Christ might be magnified through the life of the Saint. Some of the things that happen to us are bad, but with the power of the Holy Ghost at work in the situation, God can enable us to get good out of bad.

This Week's Objective:
In all things, give thanks and continue to minister and to magnify Christ.

BLINDED MINDS

But if our gospel be hid, it is hid to them that are lost: In whom the god of this world hath blinded the minds of them which believe not, lest the light of the glorious gospel of Christ, who is the image of God, should shine unto them.

—2 Corinthians 4:3–4 (KJV)

Reflection: *Sin separates people from God.*

OR SOME REASON, MANY ASSOCIATE BEING SAVED WITH A DRAB, monotonous, and boring way of life. Many men think that Christianity, and I don't mean this from a homosexual's viewpoint, is for sissies and that real men do not need God. However, the Bible tells us that there is joy in serving the Lord. The joy of the Lord is your strength. The unsaved are blind to the joys of sonship. They do not recognize how wonderful it is to be a child of God. I'm so glad that I know Him, because He knows the way that I take. And when things get rough, He's always there to give me direction.

The devil blinds the minds of people to the terrible consequences of sin and to their need for salvation. From the beginning of human history, Satan has sought to create the impression that sin is not that serious. In the Garden of Eden, the serpent said in Genesis 3:4, "Ye shall not surely die," implying that sin is not bad enough to cause you to die. The devil will use many things to blindfold you from seeing your need for the grace of God. It is time for you to cast off these blindfolds and come face to face with your need for the forgiveness of sin and the gift of spiritual life through faith in Christ Jesus.

My friends, you must see past the minor difficulties that are placed in your life. A man in the Bible named Job declared that because of what he had been through, he was able to see God through his spiritual vision. Once the blindfolds have been removed, you can see the invisible, expect the impossible, and feel the intangible.

Do you need help in putting off the blindfold that Satan has placed on your mind? If so, then try to evaluate your life in comparison, not with those who have failed to be genuinely Christian, but with the finest Christian you have ever known. Look at the cross and see how Jesus suffered and died so that He might be your Savior. Contemplate the issues and the values of eternity. Recognize the emptiness and incompleteness of your life without God. Face up to the fact that without God, the influence of your life will be such as to lead others away from God. Become aware of the brevity of life and the certainty of death. As these thoughts penetrate, they can help you to throw off the blindfolds so that the light of the glorious gospel of Christ can shine.

This Week's Objective:
Salvation is the gift of God.

THE SPIRIT FOR RENEWAL

And be not conformed to this world: but be ye transformed
by the renewing of your mind, that ye may prove what *is*
that good, and acceptable, and perfect, will of God.

—Romans 12:2 (KJV)

Not by works of righteousness which we have done, but
according to His mercy He saved us, by the washing
of regeneration, and renewing of the Holy Ghost.

—Titus 3:5 (KJV)

Reflection: *People should always walk after the Spirit.*

THE KEY TO RENEWAL IS NOT OUR PLANS, OUR PROGRAMS, OR OUR techniques; rather, it is the person of the Holy Spirit. There is an apparent absence of the Holy Spirit in the life of the church and an apparent ignorance of His ministry. What do you know about the Holy Spirit and His ministry in your life?

The Spirit enters the life of a person after he or she accepts the Lord as Savior. The death, burial, and resurrection of Jesus provides the means of salvation and the Holy Ghost effects it. He convicts us of our need for salvation (John 16:8). He regenerates us in salvation (John 3:6–7). He takes up residence within us (John 14:16–17; Romans 8:9). And He seals us to the day of redemption. He is our assurance of salvation (Ephesians 1:13–14).

The indwelling of the Holy Ghost is a term that refers to the control of the Spirit. Ephesians 5:18 says, "Be not drunk with wine, wherein is excess; but be filled with the Spirit." This analogy between alcoholic intoxication and being filled with the Spirit describes the situation that occurs when one is filled with wine. It means that every part of a person's body is affected: how he or she walks, talks, thinks, and sees. It is the idea of control.

When the Holy Ghost is in control, something happens in our lives. He delivers us from the defeat of self (Romans 7:8–25). He cultivates Christ-like qualities (Galatians 5:22–23). He teaches us (1 Corinthians 2:9–10). He leads us (Roman 8:14). He assures us (Romans 8:16). He strengthens us (Ephesians 3:16). He empowers us for witnessing (Acts 1:8).

The Spirit-filled life is a life of faith. We are saved by faith, we live by faith, we walk by faith, and we are filled with the Holy Ghost by faith—not by feelings, but by faith.

It is impossible for us as saints to produce power and Christ-like qualities apart from being controlled by the Holy Ghost. We must decide to live Spirit-filled lives. We must allow the Holy Ghost to have us. It is an act of our will, and it is a continual experience.

This Week's Objective:
Let us be done with doubting. Let us trust God's Word for the Holy Ghost.

WHAT A FOOL BELIEVES

The pride of thine heart hath deceived thee, thou that dwellest
in the clefts of the rock, whose habitation *is* high; that saith
in his heart, Who shall bring me down to the ground?
—Obadiah 1:3 (KJV)

Reflection: *Pride comes before a fall.*

I F AT ANY TIME WE MUST TAKE AN INVENTORY OF OURSELVES, IT MUST BE now. The Bible tells us that from the heart flows the issues of life. We cannot fool our hearts with our outward performance. If we think we are being successful at the game we are playing, we are being deceived by our hearts. This is true of all proud persons, for pride is what a fool believes. As you examine yourself to reach the conclusion that you are not proud, be careful. Those who are sure that they have no pride are probably the proudest of all. I must tell you that pride is the beginning of a tremendous downfall.

In our Scripture, we have the descendants of Esau, called Edom. They were well-learned men and were the heads of governments. History tells us these people were the grandeurs of society; their hearts told them they were all that. Edom, because of their high-mindedness, made a bold statement: "Who shall bring me down to the ground?" Many people today have this same type of attitude. They speak with confidence of their own strength.

Carnal security easily besets people in the days of their pomp, power, glory, and prestige. Carnal security ripens people for ruin and aggravates it when it comes. What does God say to Edom? The vision that Obadiah has is that God will destroy Edom, and this vision, or rather this order, is irreversible. If people are foolish enough to challenge the omnipotence of God, their challenge shall be taken up. In other words, if you are stupid enough to sell (let me put it in modern day language) wolf tickets, God is bad enough to buy all of them. "Who shall bring me down?" says Edom. God replies, "I will!" God says it is only thy imagination running away with you.

You think you're fooling God, but that is only what a fool believes. You've built your confidence in materialism and in your alliances in an effort to get to the top. Rich relatives, influential friends, tried allies—all will fail those who trust in them. In every way, pride lays a person open to being deceived. The person's judgment is perverted by pride and pride will lead that person into evil ways. Pride will cause one to show contempt of holy things and will secure his or her ruin.

We must not put confidence in ourselves. As 1 Corinthians 10:12 says, "Wherefore let him that thinketh he standeth take heed lest he fall." It's a danger to think you can make it on your own. Proverbs 28:26 tells us, "He that trusteth in his own heart is a fool; but whoso walketh wisely shall be delivered."

This Week's Objective:
Examine yourself often and be set free.

WHEN TROUBLE COMES

I will lift up my eyes unto the hills, from whence cometh my help.
My help cometh from the Lord, which made heaven and earth.

—Psalm 121:1–2 (KJV)

Reflection: *The only true source of help and strength is God.*

IN ACHIEVING SERENITY OF LIFE ON EARTH IN THE FACE OF TROUBLES, A person must look and see the Lord in the glory of the star-lit heavens. Then, we can answer our own question concerning the origin of our help: "My help cometh from the Lord, which made heaven and earth."

It has often been said that a person needs to occasionally remove himself or herself from his or her usual scene of activity in order to obtain a truly objective view of a situation. Certainly, we need to look away from our troubles to the source of all help before we turn back to face them. The psalmist took a long look at the distant hills and at the Lord of the hills; then he turned back to analyze his problems. Somehow, as he looked at his trouble with eyes of faith, his whole perspective changed; each problem seemed to fall into its proper place.

The passing of the years has a way of teaching that things are not always as they appear. Events along life's way that at first appeared to be the greatest of catastrophes turned out to be, or were converted into, the greatest of life's opportunities. In looking over biblical history and world history, we are able to cite many examples where this was so. No matter what you are going through, learn how to take those lemons and turn them into lemonade.

A person whose heart is bound in faith to the Master grows and develops through the difficulties and troubles that the Lord uses as stepping stones for growth in grace and knowledge of Him. Until a person has gone through the fiery trials of life, that person has not known the strength that comes from God.

As Christians, we live each day fully dependent on the leadership of the Master. We do so in faith, believing that the Master will give us strength for that day. We trust God alone to save us, and trust is literally faith in action. You may have a great intellectual belief in Jesus, but until you have acted on that belief, you have not come to the point of trusting Him.

When life falls in on you and it seems impossible for you to bear, turn your eye upon the Lord from whence cometh your help. Look to Him in faith, believing that He has the power to undergird you and to strengthen you to face life.

This Week's Objective:
Look outside yourself for help; exercise faith and trust in God.

CAN WE SURVIVE?

I will not die, but live, and declare the works of the Lord.
—Psalms 118:17 (KJV)

Reflection: *God is a protector.*

"**C**AN WE SURVIVE?" IS A QUESTION ASKED BY MANY PEOPLE TODAY. IN a society that is disgruntled by bleakness and shame, in a world that is scorched by the burning suns of trials and pestilence, and in a civilization that is bombarded by the falling rocks of mutilated humanity, we must grapple with the question, "Can we survive?" With each new day that dawns, we stand on the brink of nonexistence.

In America, unemployment figures are staggering; even more Americans have been forced to live in subhuman environments. Modern-day sociologists have painted a shocking scenario. They tell us that, with the rapid advance of the technological age, it is possible that we are developing a permanent underclass of uneducable, unskilled, and unemployable citizens.

The present administration has budgeted monies in excess to increase the nation's military strength. We are told that other nations have developed weapons of mass destruction (WMDs), which, if they are not dismantled, will cause a nuclear holocaust with the ability to eliminate humankind. My question becomes even more prevalent: "Can we survive?" We are continuously frightened by the fierce determination for global superiority that this nation pursues. We're guilty of shoving our imperialistic weight around to perhaps gain control of the world.

However, the biblical record announces with poignant clarity that it is not always the fittest that will reach the mark and gain the prize. When we were weak, without strength, and in a state of passive helplessness to deliver ourselves from sin, Christ died. At the time in our lives when we were completely disqualified from real existence, Christ died for us. Now, because of Jesus Christ, we can survive. God rises up and fights on the side of the weak, the disadvantaged, and the oppressed. He gives no preferential attention to the high and mighty, but has earnest compassion for the meek and lowly.

In spite of how things may look, be sure that you're viewing the big picture. You are already a survivor and you have already won. God has given you the victory. Can we survive? The answer is an unequivocal yes. The storms of life may rise, but God will make a way for your escape.

This Week's Objective:
Trust in God and don't worry about the prognosticators.

DRAWING WATER FROM THE RIGHT WELLS

Therefore with joy shall ye draw water
out of the wells of salvation.

—Isaiah 12:3 (KJV)

Reflection: *There is a well that never runs dry.*

GOD'S WONDERFUL PROVISIONS THROUGH JESUS CHRIST ARE DESCRIBED as being comparable to wells of living water in a hot, dry country where water is scarce. This land in which we live is a parched land when it comes to godliness. We have drifted to spiritual neglect, self-indulgence, and permissiveness. The prophet Jeremiah was grieved because the people of his nation had forsaken God, who was the fountain of living waters, and had hewn out for themselves broken cisterns that could not hold water.

God is no cistern. A cistern is a tank used for the collection and storage of rainwater for times of drought, constructed by human effort, limited in both quantity and capacity, and subject to leakage and destruction. On the other hand, God's great salvation is described as a flowing stream, as an artesian well. The water is always fresh, free, abundant in supply, and health giving.

The word *wells* is being used in the plural. You can draw water from the well of forgiveness or from the well of your new relationship with God, our loving Father. You can draw water from the well of the promise of the Savior's personal presence, the indwelling Spirit of the Holy Ghost, which has come to be your companion. You can draw water from the well of family relationships and in the privilege of being a part of the family of God. You can draw water from the well of assurance that when this life is over, you have a house not made with hands, eternal in the heavens. With joy, we are to draw water from the wells of salvation.

When it comes to the matter of salvation, each of us must draw his or her own water. We must recognize and respond to the resources God makes available. Realize you will only find joy in the sweet-smelling Savior, the Lily of the Valley, and the Bright and Morning Star. You can only find real joy in Jesus. Jesus says that if you come unto Him, He will in no wise cast you out. Love, joy, peace, and hope are to be found only as we draw water from the wells of salvation.

The words of our scriptural text should bring us great personal encouragement. They should assure us that Jesus will be present in our every time of need. The challenge of our text is very personal in application. You must sleep your own sleep. You must eat your own food. You must do your own rejoicing in the Lord, and all of us must draw our own water from the wells of salvation.

This Week's Objective:
Let Christ come into your heart and bring you the living water of life.

THANKS, BUT NO THANKS. I NEED GOD FOR THIS ONE

Give us help from trouble: for vain is the help of man.
—Psalms 60:11 (KJV)

Reflection: *The strength of God helps us conquer all.*

THERE ARE SOME HARDSHIPS AND DIFFICULTIES THAT HUMANS CANNOT help us get through. Instead of seeking the aid of fallible human beings, learn how to go to that Rock that is higher than yourself. We appreciate offered assistance and encouraging words from family and friends, but every now and then we have to say, "Thanks, but no thanks. I'm going to need God for this one." Trouble is sometimes born out of the problems of life and, in many cases, born out of a rebellious spirit toward God. Sometimes, trouble is accompanied with fretfulness and impatience. At times people contend with it in a spirit of self-sufficiency and rely on their own ingenuity. Our text contains a very striking and affecting prayer. It is one that all will be called on to offer at one time or another. Happy is it when sorrow leads to prayer, and affliction to a more devoted and spiritual life. It was the psalmist who said it had been good for me to be afflicted that I might learn thy statutes.

Humans are very limited in their capabilities. Good people may give wise counsel, and they may sympathize sincerely and tenderly, but they cannot sustain us in trouble, sanctify our sorrows, or deliver us out of our afflictions. People cannot control our circumstances, drive back our enemies, or turn our afflictions into blessings—but God can. The Bible says, "That He will, with the temptation, make a way for our escape." He was help to the children of Israel on the way to the Red Sea, and help to Daniel in the lions' den. He helped Meshach, Shadrach, and Abednego in the fiery furnace. He was help for Paul and Silas who were locked in jail. God was help for humankind by rescuing our souls from a burning hell. "Oh, what a friend we have in Jesus, all of our sins and grieves to bare. Oh, what a privilege it is to carry everything to God in prayer."

"The name of God is a strong tower the righteous runneth into it and are safe," states Proverbs 18:10. He will be bread in a starving land and water in dry places. God is a very present help in the time of trouble. We need Him at all times, but especially in our days and nights of struggle. Somebody is in trouble today and looking for deliverance through people, but only God can do it.

This Week's Objective:
Go to God concerning all of your troubles. He will deliver.

UNCONTROLLED APPETITES

The Lord is my shepherd; I shall not want.

—Psalm 23:1 (KJV)

Reflection: The Lord shows His people the right way.

S OMEONE SUGGESTED THAT THERE ARE FEW PERFECT CREATIONS IN THE world. Among those characterized as near-perfect are the Taj Mahal, the Parthenon, the Sistine Chapel, and the Twenty-third Psalm. Nothing else written by people is known by as many persons as is this psalm. "The Lord is my shepherd," has provided hope, health, and happiness literally to multitudes, who are not ashamed to identify themselves as the sheep of the Lord's pasture. Yet, there are many misapplications and misinterpretations of this same psalm. Let us take a brief look at what this passage really says and means. I attempt to show how the appetite can be out of control and not in line with what God would have.

The appetite that says, "The Lord is my Shepherd; I can have anything that I want" is a response flowing from a purely Americanized and Westernized theology of materialism: cars, credit cards, and condominiums. There are those who would have us believe that God is like a genie in a bottle. If we rub Him the right way, we can have anything we want. But what about Psalm 37:4, which says, "Delight thyself also in the Lord; and he shall give thee the desires of thine heart." When you delight yourself in Him, He regulates your desires. God is not a pawn in your hand. Because the Lord is your shepherd does not mean you can manipulate Him and have anything you want. Some things we want are not good for us, but every good and perfect gift comes from God.

"The Lord is my shepherd I shall not want." This is the response that flows out of a relationship with God. It affects my affections and my attitude. One thing we need to remember about sheep is that they do not go searching for greener pastures on their own. They do not concern themselves with where they grazed yesterday or where they will graze tomorrow. Their only concern is with where is the shepherd, because they know that He will lead them beside the still waters. It is only as we live in proper relationship to Him in the now that we can say, "The Lord is my shepherd, I shall not want." David the king learned this lesson well. He gave us the foundation for his faith in Psalm 37:25: "I have been young, and now am old; yet have I not seen the righteous forsaken, nor his seed begging bread." David was now an old man, but he had come to the sunset years of his life saying, "The Lord is my shepherd, I shall not want." His statement was the declaration of a made-up mind; he refused to be in want.

Which response is for you? As for me, I choose that of a made-up mind steadfast in the knowledge that the Lord truly is my shepherd and I shall not want. He will make a way for me. He will open doors. He will keep me and guide me.

This Week's Objective:
Be content hearing the voice of God.

WHAT IF? A HORRIBLE HYPOTHETICAL SITUATION

If Christ be not risen, then is our preaching
vain, and your faith is also vain.

—1 Corinthians 15:14 (KJV)

Reflection: *Jesus Christ lives.*

THIS MESSAGE IS NOT AN EFFORT TO PROVE THAT CHRIST AROSE BUT TO proclaim that He is risen. The proof of the risen Lord cannot be substantiated by mere words; the authenticity of a risen Lord must be accepted by faith. The apostle Paul anticipated an argument that, had it been valid, would destroy the foundation of Christianity. With his keen logical mind, Paul saw that if there were no such thing as a resurrection of the dead, then the glorious news that Christ is alive must be labeled as false and untrustworthy. Paul presents the most horrible hypothesis that hell could ever manufacture in order to set the scene for an examination of the consequences, thus testing the validity of such a claim.

What if Christ is not risen? Then our personal faith and witnessing is meaningless. Think for a moment of the great preachers who have lived through the centuries: Charles Spurgeon in London, C. H. Mason in Mississippi, David Livingstone in Germany, and many, many others. If Christ did not rise, then all of these men were fools, they were duped by their own egos, and they wasted their lives. In our own day, revivals and church services are not only a waste of time and money, but are actually propagations of false doctrine. What if Christ did not rise? Then these terrible things are true and we are guilty of being foolish fanatics.

Every effort that we have made to win the lost to Christ has been only foolishness and vanity if Christ did not get up out of the grave. In addition, we have received no true forgiveness because the price for our redemption has not been justified. We are, of all people, most miserable if Christ is not risen. Thank God that, even in our worst anticipation, some things are yet true. Hell's most horrible hypothesis fails the test of experience and validity. The satanic forces have done their best to persuade the world, but the evidence is irrefutable. The resurrection is true.

Christ is risen. We must reiterate that the purpose of this message is not to prove, but to proclaim. Others have proven; read their works, study the evidence, but then remember one thing: you cannot be saved by believing with your head. You must accept the truth with your heart, which means full commitment to the resurrected Christ. When the resurrection is accepted by faith, a power comes into our lives that is impossible in any other way. Jesus is alive; an empty tomb is there to prove our Savior lives. Thank God for the victory we have in Jesus.

This Week's Objective:
Tell the world that it's not just a story, but it's reality. He lives.

DON'T BE SURPRISED WHEN GOD ANSWERS YOUR PRAYERS

Peter therefore was kept in prison: but prayer was made without ceasing of the church unto God for him. And as Peter knocked at the door of the gate, a damsel came to hearken, named Rhoda. And when she knew Peter's voice, she opened not the gate for gladness, but ran in, and told how Peter stood before the gate. And they said unto her, Thou art mad. But she constantly affirmed that it was even so. Then said they, It is his angel.

—Acts 12:5, 13–16 (KJV)

Reflection: *Through prayer, God's will is manifested.*

PRAYER IS AN EXPRESSION OF SINCERE DESIRE. WE MUST NOTE THAT prayer is not to inform God of matters that He would otherwise be ignorant of. The validity of prayer is not affected by its length or repetitiveness. Answered prayer involves sincerity and an unwavering commitment to our personal relationships with God. When things happen to us, we pray and say that we believe, but in actuality we don't think God is going to come through on our behalf. Praying in the will of God changes things, people, and situations. The apostle Peter was imprisoned by King Herod and placed under the guard of sixteen soldiers. Herod's intention was to deliver Peter to the Jews for execution after the Passover, "but prayer was made without ceasing of the Church unto God for him."

God works in mysterious ways. The night before Peter was to be executed, suddenly there was a light in the cell and an angel of the Lord hit Peter on the side and said, "Wake up!" When Peter stood, the chains fell off his wrists. Peter thought he was dreaming and did not believe the reality of what was occurring. Peter and the angel walked out of the prison toward an iron gate and it opened of its own accord. The angel disappeared. Peter said, "Now I know of a surety, that the Lord hath sent His angel, and hath delivered me out of the hand of Herod, and from all the expectation of the people of the Jews." The saints' prayers were answered.

Peter went to Mary's house. When a damsel named Rhoda recognized Peter's voice, she left Peter outside, and ran to tell everyone that Peter was at the door. They didn't believe and said, "Thou art mad." When Rhoda insisted, they said, "It is his angel." When they finally opened the door, they were surprised and amazed.

Why are you praying if you don't think God can make a way and bring you out? The Bible says that the effectual fervent prayers of a righteous person availeth much. Prayer still works. Please don't be surprised; God is getting ready to answer your prayer. First John 3:22 says, "And whatsoever we ask, we receive of him, because we keep his commandments, and do those things that are pleasing in his sight."

This Week's Objective:
Believe and dance in advance. God is working in your favor.

BE CAREFUL WHO KEEPS YOU WARM

Then took they him, and led him, and brought him into the high priest's house. And Peter followed afar off. And when they had kindled a fire in the midst of the hall, and were set down together, Peter sat down among them.

–Luke 22:54-55 (KJV)

Reflection: No good ever comes from giving in to weaknesses.

IT IS SO EASY TO THINK THAT WE ARE STRONGER THAN WE REALLY ARE. Be careful, I Corinthians 10:12 says, "Therefore let him who thinks he stands take heed lest he fall." No saint is immune to "the flaming arrows of the evil one" (Ephesians 6:16). The devil doesn't care about your anointing or your position in the church. He's persistent and will monitor your behavior so he can catch you at a weak moment. Peter was blind to his own weakness. He confidently told the Lord in Luke 22:23 that, "I am ready to go with you to prison and to death." This was a noble expression and a wonderful assurance, apparently uttered in ignorance of his fleshly potential for succumbing to sin's temptation. Satan, the evil one, caught the strong disciple in a vulnerable moment—surrounded by the enemy and separated from the other disciples.

Peter was a strong individual, a great leader, and a dynamic Christian. In spite of all these great qualities, Peter denied the Lord. I must caution you that when there is a call upon your life, you need not feel bad because you are alone. The anointing has a way of alienating you from people who are not spiritual. But the pressure to conform and be guided by others can be intense. Remember your "struggle is not against flesh and blood, but against the rulers, against the authorities, against the powers of this dark world, and against the spiritual forces of evil in the heavenly realms" (Matthew 6:13). Be careful who you keep warm with, and carefully examine who you associate with and tell your secrets to.

Peter was guilty of trying to keep warm by the enemy's fire. He was afraid to resist the pressure of people, even though they were against God. What are you to do in the face of pressure from those around you? Paul says to do what is pleasing to God in Romans 12:2, "And do not be conformed to this world, but be transformed by the renewing of your mind, that ye may prove what is that good and acceptable and perfect will of God." If you're going to succeed in life, know the temper and spirit of the times in which you live and act accordingly. Walk with God and take on a new outlook. Choose to be cold externally and feel the warmth of God on the inside rather than be warm at the enemy's fire.

This Week's Objective:
Walk and live in the warmth of the love of God.

JUDGE NOT

"Judge not that ye be not judged."

—Matthew 7:1 (KJV)

Reflection: *Words spoken mirror the soul.*

VOTERS MUST JUDGE BETWEEN CANDIDATES AND PLATFORMS. A JUDGE on a bench must judge the innocence or guilt of an accused person. We must all participate in some kind of judgment. What then does our Lord mean when he says, "Judge not"? Did Jesus prohibit discernment? Our Lord is not teaching that the Christian should never express his or her opinion of others. He indicates that the Christian must be able to discern between those classified as dogs and hogs. He says in Matthew 7:6, "Give not that which is holy unto the dogs, neither cast ye your pearls before swine, lest they trample them under their feet, and turn again and rend you."

Jesus also indicates that the Christian should be able to discriminate between a false and a true prophet as found in Matthew 7:15–20:

> "Beware of false prophets, which come to you in sheep's clothing, but inwardly they are ravening wolves. Ye shall know them by their fruits. Do men gather grapes of thorns, or figs of thistles? Even so every good tree bringeth forth good fruit; but a corrupt tree bringeth forth evil fruit. A good tree cannot bring forth evil fruit, neither can a corrupt tree bring forth good fruit. Every tree that

bringeth not forth good fruit is hewn down, and cast into the fire. Wherefore by their fruits ye shall know them."

The Christian should be able to discriminate between true and false teachings (Galatians 1:8), detect error (2 Timothy 2:16–18), and detect and eliminate heresy (Titus 3:10).

However, beware of the marks of a critical person. Christians should not delight in the criticism and condemnation of others. One of the most horrible traits in many Christians' lives is the critical spirit. The Bible teaches, "If any man among you seem to be religious, and bridleth not his tongue…this man's religion is vain" (James 1:26).

Those who gripe the most at work, at home, or at church usually do the least. They gripe to cover up their laziness, unfaithfulness, sin, backsliding, and mistakes. The critical person criticizes personalities and disregards principles. They express opinions without knowing all of the facts. It has been said that a faultfinder is never a good factfinder.

The Bible says, "Do not judge according to appearance, but judge with righteous judgment" (John 7:24). Subduing a critical spirit begins with harnessing what we think. Practice Philippians 4:8: "Finally, brethren, whatsoever things are true, whatsoever things are honest, whatsoever things are just, whatsoever things are pure, whatsoever things are lovely, whatsoever things are of good report; if there be any virtue, and if there be any praise, think on these things."

This Week's Objective:
Refuse to be critical of others. Find real happiness.

LIFE IN A CROOKED WORLD

That ye may be blameless and harmless, the sons of God,
without rebuke, in the midst of a crooked and perverse
nation, among whom ye shine as lights in the world.

—Philippians 2:15 (KJV)

Reflection: How we live matters.

THE SAINT OF GOD MUST LIVE A LIFE THAT IS NOT CONTRADICTORY TO the established Word of God. Today, people are constantly finding excuses not to serve God and reasons to be rebellious. We are argumentative and consistently looking for the least intrusive way to live saved. However, we should be constantly trying to make sure that the world does not find reasons to discredit our walks with Christ. Paul said if we are to be who Christ is calling for, in these last and evil days, we must be blameless and innocent. Paul told the church at Ephesus, "For ye were sometimes darkness, but now light in the Lord: walk as children of light" (Ephesians 5:8).

Salvation or being saved is more than a label that we wear; it is a lifestyle. Many will not be numbered among those who are saved because of selfish ambition, arrogance, or conceit. Others may not be considered saints because they are not willing to discipline themselves. Living a humble and obedient life is a mandate for those who profess Christ. Because of Christ's humility and willingness to place our lives ahead of His, God has made it so that at His very name, every knee shall bow and every tongue must confess that He is Lord.

Saints are to be harmless as doves in their imitation of Jesus Christ. Christ was holy in His nature and harmless in His conversation and, as His followers, we should be the same. We should not do harm to any person, not to his or her property. We should not behave in an offensive manner to anyone. We should act like children of God. Our character and behavior as saints make us children of God. It testifies to the world that an encounter with Jesus changes one's behavior. "Therefore, if any man be in Christ Jesus, he is a new creature: old things are passed away; behold, all things are become new" (2 Corinthians 5:17).

The churches of Christ are as candlesticks, in which the light of the Gospel is lit, and held forth for people to see. The world is watching us and we should not give them any reasons to be correct in their rebuke. When the light comes on, you avoid the snares of the devil and of life. The saints are the lights of the world. We were once a part of darkness, but now we have become light by the Lord Jesus Christ.

This Week's Objective:
Demonstrate you are a partaker of God's divine
nature through a disciplined walk with God.

LODEBAR IS NOT A PLACE FOR ROYALTY

And the king said unto him, Where is he? And Ziba said unto
the king, Behold, he is in the house of Machir, the son of
Ammiel, in Lodebar. Then King David sent, and fetched him
out of the house of Machir, the son of Ammiel, from Lodebar.

— Samuel 9:4–5 (KJV)

Reflection: The place where you live is not
always reflective of who you are.

L IFE CAN TAKE MANY DIFFERENT TURNS, SOME OF WHICH LEAVE US displaced and debilitated. Things happen along life's journey that we will never forget because they have left indelible impressions on our lives. However, there comes a time when we have to realize who we are and not be hindered by our pasts. No matter what life has dictated up to this point and regardless of what we are experiencing at the moment, there is no time to sulk. God can always make a way to escape. Let us look at a situation in the life of a royal prince called Mephibosheth that gives us hope.

As the grandson of King Saul, Mephibosheth had the luxury of having a nurse to take care of him. That nurse dropped Mephibosheth and, as a result, he was lame in both feet. After the mishap, Mephibosheth's nurse carried him to a lowly place called Lodebar. Sometimes circumstances dictate that we live in Lodebar, but at other times, we have adjusted ourselves to believing that we can do no better. Mephibosheth became a product of his environment, resigned in his mind that this was the way he was supposed to live.

People today seem to possess a state of mind that accepts living in downtrodden situations, having nothing, and going nowhere. Have you become acclimated to your surroundings and resigned yourself to perpetual irrelevance and sorrow? No matter how deplorable things have become in your life or how you came to reside in Lodebar, you are royalty and Lodebar is not a place for you. Mephibosheth was eventually invited to dine at the royal table because God reminded King David of his commitment to his friend Jonathan, Mephibosheth's father. God has a plan for your life and a promise has been made on your behalf. God is saying, "Come sit at my table."

God has purpose for your life and there is hope for your future. You cannot do what God wants done in a Lodebar state of mind. Stop reliving the hurts of the past, stop wallowing in misfortunes, and stop wailing over the abuse and misuse experienced. The Bible says, "God has made us what we are. He has created us in Christ Jesus to live lives filled with good works that He has prepared for us to do." You are royalty and joy, happiness, healing and redemption is yours. God said in Ezekiel 36:11, "I will make you better off than ever before. Then you will know that I am the Lord."

This Week's Objective:
God has turned your situation around and He will take care of you.

THE YEAR OF MANIFESTATION

Then Isaac sowed in that land, and received in the same
year a hundredfold: and the Lord blessed him.

—Genesis 26:12 (KJV)

Reflection: *God cannot lie. He is true to His word.*

THE DELAYED MANIFESTATION OF OUR PROMISES IS NOT DUE TO ANY lack on God's part. It is, without a doubt, the unwillingness or what may seem to be the inability by us to meet the prerequisites that God has set for us. Regardless of how we may feel, God is not going to give the promised blessings until the appropriate time. As stated in Exodus 9:5, "And the Lord appointed a set time, saying, tomorrow the Lord shall do this thing in the land." Many of us are collecting one prophetic word after another and never experiencing the manifestation of those prophesies. I believe in prophecy. I believe that God indeed has blessings for me that will change my whole perspective about life. Therefore, I am going to stand until I receive all that God promised me.

Are you really ready for the manifestation of God's word? If so, be prepared to say, "Whatever it takes, I am willing." If that means a change in attitude or cutting ties with the past, you must be ready. If you are honestly feeling anxious and frustrated because of the wait, let me encourage you. God indeed has a promised land for you.

One lesson conveyed in the Scriptures is the continuation of God's faithfulness. It is very easy to become discouraged when prophecies don't come to fruition right away. If we are not careful, we will find ourselves flirting with the possibility of regression. Don't go to the right or the left; just stand still and delight yourself in the promise that God made to you. Worship and praise God as though the manifestation of His word in your life has already been received. A part of learning to trust God is walking by faith and not by sight.

In the face of impending famine, the Lord promised to be with Isaac, to bless him, and to bring about all that had been promised to his father, Abraham. Essentially the same promise given to Abraham was given to his son, Isaac. Here is the beginning of the manifestation of God's promise in Isaac's life. The Bible says, "Then Isaac sowed in that land, and received in the same year a hundredfold, and the Lord blessed him." Isaac became very progressive, very great, and very rich. Isaac, in that year, became so blessed that the Philistines envied him.

God has promised to manifest blessings in your life that are undeniably yours and uniquely belong to you. Manifestation is going to be so obvious that no one will be able to deny God's hand is on you. God promised some things a long time ago, and they are about to be manifested.

This Week's Objective:
Get ready! God is turning things around for you.

THE HOLY GHOST AS A COUNSELOR, TEACHER, AND REMINDER

"But the Counselor, the Holy Spirit, whom the Father will send in my name, he will teach you all things, and bring to your remembrance all that I have said to you."

—John 14:26 (KJV)

Reflection: The work of the Holy Ghost.

NOTHING IS MORE SATISFYING THAN THAT CLIMACTIC MOMENT IN AN individual's life when he or she discovers that God is love and that His love is expressed in His Son, Jesus Christ. Because of that discovery, one accepts Jesus Christ as personal Savior and Lord. Thereafter exists a need for consistent spiritual growth for the development of a quality saint. The method by which God grows His people is in the ministry of the Holy Ghost.

The Holy Ghost moves a holy, all-powerful God toward sinful people. Simultaneously, He moves sinful people toward God. In the indescribable glory of this miracle, the Holy Ghost brings about the new birth. He moves over the sinner, who is dead in trespasses and sins, and brings life. The Holy Ghost then continues to work with God's people.

Pentecost means fiftieth and is the day commemorating the descent of the Holy Spirit on followers of Jesus after the Resurrection. As described in Acts 2:2, "And suddenly there came a sound as of a rushing mighty wind, and it filled all the house where they were sitting." Three major things regarding the Holy Ghost happened on Pentecost. First, He became the resident presence of God in the world. His habitation became the bodies of believers, whom Paul called "temples" of the Holy Ghost (Corinthians 3:16). Second, the formation of a new body, the Church, which Jesus had promised, began. The Holy Spirit adds to this body as individuals receive Christ as Savior. Third, at Pentecost, the Holy Ghost empowered believers to witness and to share the reality of their faith with boldness and assurance.

There is no way that people can know they are lost and in need of a savior apart from the Holy Ghost, who opens their eyes to this fact. The Scripture teaches that the lost person is "dead" in sin. The Holy Spirit awakens in the lost person the first recognition of God and awareness of personal sinfulness. He reveals God's will to them and makes the Scriptures come alive and speak to their hearts. He works through their consciences to reveal truth and to encourage right decisions. The Holy Spirit is the constant companion, supporter, and guide of the saints. The Holy Ghost also constantly reveals to the believer more and more about God, His love, His purpose for the human race, and His purpose in the believer's life. He refines, teaches, encourages, and tenderly reworks.

This Week's Objective:
Believe and be filled with the Holy Ghost.

WILL SOMEBODY PLEASE PASS THE SALT?

"Ye are the salt of the earth: but if the salt have lost his savor, wherewith shall it be salted? it is thenceforth good for nothing, but to be cast out, and to be trodden under foot of men."

—Matthew 5:13

> *Reflection: An obligation lies upon all Christians to be that which salt symbolizes.*

SALT WAS TAKEN BY THE ANCIENTS AS AN EMBLEM OF WIT AND WISDOM, but Christ gave it a larger and deeper meaning. He described it as the features and elements which should characterize His disciples and make them useful to others. Salt has power to prevent the progress of corruption. That is what Jesus had in mind when He said to His disciples, "Ye are the salt of the earth." They were salt because they had been seasoned with grace, salted with the purifying fire of the Holy Ghost, and they were capable of imparting a savor of incorruption to the lost.

To be identified as the salt of the earth is the highest sense of human usefulness. It is the purpose which the Lord had in view when He called us out of darkness into the kingdom of light. Christ sets forth His disciples as "salt and light," exercising an influence for good in a world gone bad. History tells us that the disciples of Christ were the salt of the Roman Empire during the evil days of its decline, and they preserved Christianity as a moral force in that society.

Today, the world is in a sad place and it is conditioned toward corruptness. If the Church loses its savor, it has no authority to put the devil in his place. We become of no use and could lose the ability to awaken and reform the world. Those who are a part of the Church and have become good for nothing must repent. We must get back to our rightful place and serve the God who delivered us. Isaiah 55:7 states, "Let the wicked forsake his way, and the unrighteous man his thoughts: and let him return unto the LORD, and he will have mercy upon him." With a full reunion to the source of the savor, a change can occur. We are now in a position to answer the cry from the world to the church: "Will somebody please pass the salt?"

Salt has to be put in the right place. Christians are not supposed to withdraw ourselves from sinners, for they are dead in trespasses and sin. The only way by which salt can purify is by being rubbed into the corrupted thing. Spiritual salt is of little value to the community as long as it is barreled up in a church. The salt must be scattered so as to touch and to season those who are rushing to moral corruption. We need to get out of the church and go into our communities and be scattered. Salt does its work by being brought into close contact with the thing which it is to work upon.

We, the Church, have the remedy so pass it on. Each of us is responsible to do more than come to church and talk about the goodness of the Lord. Are you living a godly life before men and women and talking about God in your casual conversation? The world is hungry for the Living Bread.

This Week's Objective:
Talk about Jesus, and lift Him up.

Milton Keynes UK
Ingram Content Group UK Ltd.
UKHW040415061223
433798UK00011BB/373/J

9 798886 120196